Messages for Everyone

Larry Gene Klech

Messages for Everyone
Copyright © 2018 by Larry Gene Klech

Library of Congress Control Number:		2018943202
ISBN-13:	Paperback:	978-1-64151-810-9
	PDF:	978-1-64151-811-6
	ePub:	978-1-64151-812-3
	Kindle:	978-1-64151-813-0

Printed in the United States of America

**LitFire**
PUBLISHING

LitFire LLC
1-800-511-9787
www.litfirepublishing.com
order@litfirepublishing.com

Contents

Blessings & Thanksgivings

Body of Christ

Cheating, Lying &Stealing

Criticism

Discernment

Employment

Integrity

Jesus Christ

Negativity

Obedience

Overcoming Temptation

Patience

Perseverance

Pollutions

Popularity

Population Control

Praise

Prayer

Acknowledgements

Diana and Rhonda Klech—they taught me the value of books.

Sue Aton—her idea to index the book and her assistance in categorizing proved to be invaluable.

Debbie Daniels—her encouragement helped me through my darkest days.

Keith, Pat, and Robyn Wallace—their loving concern was a demonstration of Christianity in Action

Barbara and Hugh Baird—they bought me an electric typewriter and published this book electronically. This book would not have been published without their gracious expertise and loving generosity.

Note to the Readers

It is hoped this collection of original stories, poems, and Bible commentary will shed understanding and provide encouragement.

Atheism

The Greatest Sin

A discussion arose in our Sunday school class last week. The controversy had to do with what the greatest sin is.

Many believed that murder is the worst sin. A few of us disagreed with them for this reason: Jesus taught that if we come to God with a truly repentant heart, any sin would be forgiven.

However, if we do not believe in God, then how can we receive His forgiveness? Therefore, the greatest sin is to disbelieve in God and in His Son, Jesus.

Just in Case

Formal education has become so highly prized that it has become almost an end in itself. Many who receive high degrees feel so self-sufficient that they deny the existence of their Creator. I am always slightly amused (among other things) when I meet these atheists. I am amused because I think, deep down, they are kidding themselves. The following story will illustrate:

Phyllis, wearied by her tedious tasks, sighed heavily. "Oh God," she muttered.

Maria, her companion, responded with surprise. "I thought you didn't believe in God, Phyllis!"

"I don't," she replied wearily. "But I like to cover myself . . . just in case."

Belief

What Does It Take?

What event, or chain of events, will cause a person to believe in Jesus? The following verses of scripture should prove insightful:

- John 1:43–51

- Matthew 8:23–27

- Mark 6:45–51

- John 16:29–33

- Matthew 27:50–54

- Mark 16:12–13

- Mark 16:9–11

- John 20:24–29

This collection shows that, even among those closely associated with Him, repeated proofs were necessary.

I Looked for God

I searched all over the place for God.

I looked for Him on all the popular television shows. I scanned the newspaper every day for His picture. I thought I could find Him through deep university study.

I went to many parties and social functions, hoping to meet Him. I even went to Times Square in New York on New Year's Eve. Surely, among the many, He would be there. I also attended many sporting events, in hopes of glimpsing Him on the field or in the stands.

While spending a quiet evening at home, He came to me.

Is God Still Alive?

Jason awoke rather early, one Saturday morning. He decided he would let his wife and daughter sleep a little longer. Jason got the newspaper from the front porch and began to read it. By the time he had finished reading about crime, disasters, and family strife, he began to wonder if God was paying attention to earthly affairs anymore.

After breakfast, Jason took his daughter, Tammy, to the park. They played tennis, handball, and baseball. Jason was surprised at his daughter's athletic ability. Jason's mind wandered back many years. He remembered when his daughter had to be hospitalized for serious illnesses. Jason and his wife Diana had prayed tearfully for their only daughter.

After their fun at the park, Jason and Tammy went for a walk in the wilderness. The water still flowed downstream. Plants still grew without any human intervention. Hawks still were raised into the sky by unseen hands. Songbirds made music as sweet as any choir's. The sound of Tammy's laughter was also music to Jason's ears.

On Sunday morning, Jason and his family went to church. On the church bulletin board, the title of the day's sermon was listed: "Is God Still Alive?"

Before he even heard the sermon, Jason already knew the answer . . . *yes!*

Bible

Slugging Slogans

As the thoughtless motorist pulled into a lane in traffic, an alert driver instinctively hit the brake pedal. Thanks to one driver's quick reactions, a collision was narrowly avoided.

At the next stoplight, the careful driver jumped out of his car and approached the culprit in front of him. As the careless motorist waited for the signal to change, he was aware of someone standing next to him. As the driver turned his head to make an inquiry, a large fist momentarily pressed his lips together.

"Why did you hit me?"

"Your bumper sticker gave me the idea."

"What do you mean by that?" the bleeding man asked.

"Your bumper sticker says, 'If it feels good, do it!' I knew that hitting you would feel good, so I did it."

While the preceding narrative may appear to be a fabrication, its message is painfully clear. "If it feels good, do it!" and "You only go around once" seem to promise freedom, but before we incorporate these or any other slogans into our lives, we would do well to consider the consequences.

It is also helpful to have something with which to compare them. The Bible is a very reliable one. Do you know a better one?

And the Truth Shall Set You Free

"And you shall know the truth and the truth shall set you free," says John 8:32.

If we do not know the truth, we will not be free . . . from guilt. We may then become the victim of many fallacies. If we do not read the Bible on a continuing basis, its precious truths may slip away from us.

Remember, prayer is when we talk to God; reading the Bible is when He talks to us. If (like me) you have trouble understanding the Bible, may I suggest one of the modern translations? If Bible reading is missing from our daily lives, we may replace it with more "sophisticated" substitutes. I will tell you about some of them.

1. *Careers.* Seventeen years ago, unable to relate to my religious background and undecided about what to do with my life, I decided to enlist in the United States Air Force. It was during what has become known as the Cuban Missile Crisis.

I looked forward, with great anticipation, to becoming a war hero. After four days of defending my country with a mop and a can of shoe polish, I knew I had made the wrong decision. Unfortunately, the contract I had signed was not for four days—it was for four years.

2. *Vacations.* Some have made vacations their god. I have seen people do without life's everyday need in order to have an elaborate vacation. It was hoped these vacations would somehow transform their lives. Many times, these people returned too physically and too financially depleted to meet life's constant challenges.

Other people, choosing more modest vacations, returned to work well-rested and more financially secure.

3. *Violence.* Some people feel that displays of violence make them feel free. In 1958, the Dodgers' first year in California, I became so upset over their sloppy play; I slammed my radio to the sidewalk in an effort to vent my frustration. I had delivered a lot of newspapers to buy that radio.

In 1963, still unrepentant, I threw my radio from a third-story window. A couple of hours later, I went outside. To my surprise—although the radio's pieces were scattered all over the sidewalk—it was still playing. I decided that any radio good enough to withstand such a tantrum was too valuable to relinquish. I scooped up the fragments into a paper bag and took them downtown.

After emptying the contents onto the radio repairman's workbench, he asked me what had happened. Too embarrassed to admit the truth, I told him that I had dropped it.

He must have spotted my New York accent, for he said to me, "Where did you drop it . . . the Empire State Building?"

After the Dodgers 1978 World Series debacle, I registered only silent disgust, thereby saving my family one television set.

4. *Verbal retaliation.* This form of freedom usually leads nowhere. If I were to criticize my pastor's sermon, he could just as easily criticize my writing ability (or the lack of it).

5. *Graffiti.* This is a most distasteful form of mind pollution. At work, I see everyone smiling at one another. They carry on many conversations, and there is much laughter. They all appear to be happy, well-adjusted people.

When I go to wash my hands, I see something else. I see their true feelings about life and each other written or carved into the walls.

6. *Consumerism.* During a normal workweek, our egos suffer many bruises. Some, in an effort to mollify their egos, resort to extensive shopping sprees. While this is okay once in a while, to do this habitually could lead to financial disaster.

7. *Income tax cheating.* It has become fashionable to find as many tax loopholes as possible. When Jesus's and Peter's taxes were due, Jesus sent Peter fishing. He told Peter that the first fish he would catch would have a coin in its mouth. The coin would be of a denomination sufficient to pay for both their taxes.

Peter was a fisherman by trade. That is why Jesus chose this method for him. It was a great lesson in faith. We would all do well to remember it.

8. *Images.* Most of us have grown up in the John Wayne era. As everyone knows, in a John Wayne movie, John could solve all his problems with fists or guns. Real life is not so simplistic.

Many of you ladies have been taught that the right combination of clothes, makeup, and hairstyle will attract Mr. Right. He will see to it that you both live happily ever after.

Sadly, this has proved to be the exception rather than the rule.

9. *Pornography.* If you are really free, try this exercise. The next time you are in your garage or workshop and a neighbor shows you a copy of the latest skin magazine, prove your freedom by not exhausting your supply of adjectives.

10. *Astrology.* In an effort to be free, some like to chart the course of their lives by the position of the stars at a given time. Since God created the stars, why not worship the Creator rather than the created?

11. *Activity.* Some feel that the only real way to be free is to busy themselves with endless activity. What would these people do if they were incapacitated? I wonder if they are familiar with this scripture: "Be still and know that I am God" (Ps. 46:10).

12. *Attention.* I knew a woman at work for ten years. She bedecked herself with the most garrulous combinations of clothes imaginable. When this failed to get her the attention she so desperately desired, she became a hypochondriac.

All day long, she would bend the ears of her fellow employees with her latest symptoms. If this woman knew that God pays close attention to her, she would not have resorted to this damaging, attention-getting device.

13. *Popularity.* Some feel that popularity is the way to go. To be a friend of the world is to make yourself an enemy of God. This is what the Bible has to say about worldly popularity.

14. *Material Wealth.* Some feel that enough material wealth will insure their freedom. I wonder if they remember the parable of the rich farmer.

This man had so much grain stored up that he worried about what to do with it all. He decided to tear down his storage bins and build bigger ones. He figured he could then take it easy for the remainder of his life rather than share his riches with the less fortunate.

God came to him and said, "Thou fool, your very soul will be required of you tonight. Then what will you do with all these things that you have so selfishly stored up for yourself?" (Luke 12:20).

15. *Bigger syndrome.* There is nothing wrong with getting a bigger car or a bigger house, if you need them and can afford them. However, if you want these things in order to keep up with your neighbors or relatives, stop and think what you are doing to yourself—and your family.

16. *Worry.* Some feel they can worry themselves into a state of freedom. I fall victim to this myself. I could give numerous examples, but all I will

write is this: There is a difference between worry and concern. Worry is debilitating and unproductive. Concern can be the forerunner of action.

While many of the aforementioned "substitutes" are harmless in themselves, consider what priority they should be given.

Well, why is it so important to be set free from guilt? Because while everyone would agree that sin produces guilt, it is equally true that guilt produces more sin. This is the principle that creates alcoholics, excessive gamblers, and overeaters.

The alcoholic takes a drink to ease his worry. It feels so good that he decides to have another. One leads to another, and pretty soon too many have been consumed. Upon realizing this, the alcoholic worries about it. To ease his worry, he takes another drink.

A person gambles so heavily that large debts are incurred. In order to pay these debts, the gambler decides to "go for the big kill." When he doesn't make the big kill, his debts grow larger. To ease anxiety, a person applies "salve" to the inside of his stomach. When too much has been applied, the excess poundage becomes noticeable. The excess poundage leads to further worry, and the additional worry is appeased with more salve.

And so all these patterns continue, unless a new ingredient is introduced to the situation. However, a "new ingredient" has been introduced two thousand years ago—Jesus Christ (the Way, the Truth, and the Life).

If we confess our sins, we receive forgiveness; however, we must also forgive ourselves. If we do not forgive ourselves, we are liable to punish ourselves (as some of the previously mentioned substitutes have indicated). Jesus does not want to see us punished. That is why He instituted the New Testament. The New Testament is based on internal controls rather than external controls. I will give you three examples as to why internal controls are superior to external controls.

There is a fifty-five-mile-per-hour speed limit. If anyone is caught exceeding this limit, they can receive a citation. By keeping one eye on the rearview mirror, many people are able to avoid detection.

However, when a person, guided by the right Spirit (The Holy Spirit), realizes that this limit makes the highways safer for himself and others—he obeys it, whether he is being watched or not.

I have heard parents say to their children, "I better never catch you smoking." These parents will probably never catch their children smoking. But that is not to say that their children will not smoke. They may smoke when they feel that the coast is clear.

Other parents take a different approach. In a spirit of love and reason, they explain the hazards of smoking. The latter approach usually obtains better results than the former.

For the last reason why love is superior to fear, I will use the examples of Julius Caesar and Jesus Christ.

Julius Caesar was the emperor of all the known world. Today, his kingdom has shrunk to one boot-shaped country. Jesus Christ—using no force, little money, and few followers—has lived to see His Kingdom swell to about one billion Christians.

God's Rainbow

Last week, many Southern Californians were beginning to wonder if it would ever stop raining. The week-long deluge had taken its toll in human life and property damage. In spite of the doubt-raising disasters, some people did not wonder if the rain would finally subside. They knew it would stop because God told them it would stop! In Genesis, God says,

> I will never do it again. I will never again curse the earth, destroying all living things, even though man's bent is always toward evil from his earliest youth, and even though he does such wicked things. As long as the earth remains, there will be springtime and harvest, cold and heat, winter and summer, day and night. (Gen. 8:21–22)

> Then God told Noah and his sons, "I solemnly promise you and your children and the animals you brought with you—all these birds and cattle and wild animals—that I will never again send another

flood to destroy the earth. And I seal this promise with this sign: I have placed my rainbow in the clouds as a sign of my promise until the end of time, to you and to all the earth. When I send clouds over the earth, the rainbow will be seen in the clouds, and I will remember my promise to you and to every being, that never again will the floods come and destroy all life. For I will see the rainbow in the cloud and remember my eternal promise to every being on the earth." (Gen. 9:8-17)

For more of God's promises, see the Bible.

Flip Sides

When manufacturing a record, the hit song is always accompanied by a flip side. In some cases, particularly with the more lasting artists, the flip side proves to be more durable than the hit side (after the initial fanfare subsides).

When manufacturing a philosophy based on popular Bible verses, it is even more important to learn the flip sides as well. Knowing both sides will give us a better sense of balance. The Bible is better understood in its entirety. Those who stress only the more palatable verses ignore Paul's instructions:

> You know how, when you were a small child, you were taught the holy Scriptures; and it is these that make you wise to accept God's salvation by trusting in Christ Jesus. The *whole* Bible was given to us by inspiration from God and is useful to teach us what is true and to make us realize what is wrong in our lives. It straightens us out and helps us do what is right. It is God's way of making us well-prepared at

every point, fully equipped to do good to everyone. (2 Tim. 3:15–17; italics added by the author)

The Ultimate Advice

I first met Mr. Carson when I was in high school. He quickly became my favorite teacher because he had the knack of turning even the most boring subjects into interesting classes. I knew that I would not forget him, even after graduation.

Since I did not communicate well with my own father, I started going to Mr. Carson for advice. He supplied me with timely insights at crucial times in my young life. He advised me well when I was considering running away from home. He advised me when I considered enlisting in the military.

After fulfilling military obligation, I sought out Mr. Carson for advice on reentering civilian life. One thing he told me that I'll never forget is, "Everything in life calls for a certain procedure. If you follow the right procedure, you will arrive at the right conclusion." His advice served me well for a number of years, but the day came when I needed something more.

I went to Mr. Carson and told him how unhappy I felt inside. His advice at first disappointed then puzzled me. Finally, it satisfied me so fully that I never had to seek advice from Mr. Carson again.

What did he say to me? Just this: "When you need advice, pray to the Ultimate Advisor for it. After you have asked your question, go to the Bible and receive His answers."

I followed Mr. Carson's procedure, and it has led me to the same conclusions as my former teacher. I became a Christian, like my mentor.

Now, when my Sunday school students ask for my opinion, I give the ultimate advice.

Sockin' It to 'Em

It didn't take me long to discover that I had a wife who could make anything fun. One evening, shortly after our wedding, I was in the bedroom, reading a book. My wife came in and asked if she could borrow a pair of my socks. Assuming her feet were cold, I nodded my approval.

After finishing the page, I headed for the kitchen in search of a snack. Oblivious to my presence, my wife was skating around the floor in my socks. This was her way of mopping up a spill.

Unaccustomed to this type of behavior, I continued to watch as she removed the socks and wrung them out. Then she donned them again and finished the job.

If we could all absorb the wisdom spilling out of the Bible the way a pair of socks can soak up liquid, we'd be doing all right.

Old and New Testament Parallels

While enjoying the Old Testament, you will notice some interesting parallels pointing to a new agreement between God and His people:

When the Jews painted lamb's blood on their doorframes to insure continued life for their firstborn, this was to show the Jews that they would be saved by the blood of Jesus (the Lamb of God who took away the sins of the world).

When the flood washed all sinners off the face of the earth, it was to show us that future sins would be washed away by being baptized in the name of the Lord Jesus.

Adam and Jesus represent two covenants. While Adam's failure to obey resulted in the fall of mankind, the obedience of Jesus and all those who believe in Him results in salvation.

Jonah spent three days "buried" in a big fish before delivering the Good News to the people of Nineveh; Jesus spent three days buried in the earth before giving us the Good News of his Resurrection.

Abraham became God's friend because he was willing to sacrifice his only son. We gain eternal life by believing in God's only Son, whom He sacrificed for our sake.

New Dawn

We have entered a new era of enlightenment. The more discerning religious leaders are riding a new train of thought. No longer are people being dictated to en masse. Instead, people are being given supportive guidance. Since each individual's situation is different, outdated edicts are being discarded as counterproductive.

This new dawn is promising and frightening at the same time. If people prove wise enough to base their decisions on the guidance of the Holy Spirit and God's Work, good results can be expected. However, if last week's soap opera or this month's unspiritual paperback is used as a behavioral yardstick, then deep trouble lies ahead.

Contented Cows Swallow Anything

While driving home from work today, I had the pleasure of seeing a beautiful scene. There were a dozen or so cows grazing amidst rolling green hills. While cows are admired for their qualities of contentment, this very trait has gotten many a cow into trouble. A farmer friend of mine told me how cows have been known to swallow nails, tools, barbed wire, and just about anything else lying in the grass.

In our lifetimes, we will find many opinions in the pasture of life. For this reason, we must be careful whose advice we should follow.

In the book of Acts, many people were amazed by a certain magician by the name of Simon. This magician claimed to be someone great; people from all classes of society paid close attention to him. "He is that power of God known as 'The Great Power,'" they said in Acts 8:10.

This story continues in Acts 8:12–24:

> But when they believed Philip's message
> about the good news of the Kingdom of
> God and about Jesus Christ, they were
> baptized, both men and women. Simon
> himself also believed; and after being
> baptized, he stayed close to Philip and

was astounded when he saw the great wonders and miracles that were being performed.

The apostles in Jerusalem heard that the people of Samaria had received the word of God, so they sent Peter and John to them. When they arrived, they prayed for the believers that they might receive the Holy Spirit. For the Holy Spirit had not yet come down on any of them; they had only been baptized in the name of the Lord Jesus. Then Peter and John placed their hands on them, and they received the Holy Spirit.

Simon saw that the Spirit had been given to the believers when the apostles placed their hands on them. So he offered money to Peter and John, and said: "Give this power to me too, so that anyone I place my hands on will receive the Holy Spirit."

But Peter answered him, "May you and your money go to hell, for thinking that you can buy God's gift with money! You have no part or share in our work because your heart is not right in God's sight. Repent, then, of this evil plan of yours, and pray to the Lord that he will forgive you for thinking such a thing as this. For I see that you are full of bitter envy and are a prisoner of sin."

Simon said to Peter and John, "Please pray to the Lord for me, so that none of these things you spoke of will happen to me."

So before you follow someone or accept their standards, check them against a reliable source. And what source is more reliable than the Bible? The Bible is a written record of God's word. The Bible is safe to swallow.

The Right Diet

Tina had tried to shed her excess poundage many times. Her main problem seemed to be the lack of a motivating factor. This factor was finally supplied by the attentions of a certain young man. With her newly found incentive, Tina was able to achieve her desired weight.

After her marriage, Tine decided to go on a "sin" diet. Again, the motivating force was supplied when she began to read the New Testament. When Tina realized that she always had the attention and love of God, she was able to please Him by eliminating her unspiritual excesses.

Read it Again, Sam

When a music lover hears a favorite song on the radio, he doesn't usually forget it. Instead, he often purchases a recording and enjoys listening to the song many times over. Each time he listens, the enjoyment grows deeper. Even after the words are memorized, there are vocal backgrounds and sweet notes made by various instruments to be enjoyed.

Many people think that the Bible is a book to be read only once. But to really appreciate and understand its messages, it is necessary to read it many times. Even if you have memorized all its words, there are still sweet notes between the lines that will be savored.

You Could Look It Up

Casey Stengel, the former baseball manager who led the New York Knicks in the 1950s, had a favorite ploy. When pressed by sportswriters about one issue or another, he would end the interview by stating, "You could look it up!" Casey's advice is still valid, as the following story will illustrate:

I noticed that a friend of mine seemed quite bitter about losing out on a promotion. When I asked him to air his feelings, he told me that it is God's will for Christians to be wealthy. I mentioned several verses of scripture to indicate otherwise.

He insisted that the second verse in the Third Epistle of John was the final word: "Beloved, I wish above all things that thou mayest prosper and be in health, even as thy soul prospereth" (3 John 1:2 KJV).

I suggested that John was probably not equating prosperity with material wealth. My friend became angry and accused me of being a negative thinker. After some reflection, I decided to do some research. As I had suspected, the Bible dictionary defined *prosper* (as it is used in this context) as meaning physical health.

I am sure that many sincere Christians have gone off tangent due to lack of proper reference books. To aid us in our study of God's Word, we have: Bible dictionaries, Bible encyclopedias, Bible commentaries, and topical Bibles. If the cost is prohibitive, most church libraries (and even public libraries) have them available.

A Tale of Two Men

Buck loved to hike in the wilderness. Since the winter rains, the streams had become swift and swollen. In fact, it more nearly resembled a raging river. The log that had fallen across it was not wide enough to allow for a safe crossing.

But Buck, who loved danger, decided to attempt it anyway. To improve his balance, he stretched a small log out in front of himself, à la tightrope walkers. However, the surging water had made the log slippery with its spray.

About halfway across, Buck lost his footing and tumbled into the treacherous creek. As he fell, his wooden ballast pinned him in between the log he used for a bridge. As he hung on for dear life, the coldness of the water sapped the strength from his muscles and the breath from his lungs.

"What should I do, Lord?" he cried out.

"*Let go,*" the voice inside seemed to say.

He did and was swept along swiftly through the rapids. Within a minute, however, he found himself on dry land. He was glad he had listened.

Robby loved to hike in the mountains. One day, as he was traveling his favorite trail, he stepped on a sleeping rattlesnake. Instinctively, the man jumped and slipped over the edge of a cliff.

After falling only a short distance, he managed to grab on to a small branch. It was barely larger than a twig. Knowing the piece of wood might snap at any moment, he cried out, "Help!"

Immediately, a sturdy rope was lowered to within his reach; there was Bible tied to it.

"Let go of that twig and grab on to my rope," he heard the voice command. "I will then lift you up."

But Robby was sure there must be another way. His plan was to hold out until the last possible instant. Then when he was at last convinced, he would latch on to the rope as a last resort. Before he could blink, however, the twig snapped—and he fell to his death.

Blessings
&
Thanksgivings

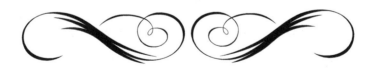

Many Happy Returns

Roy had heard that, many times, we are the recipients of our own good deeds. He decided to test this theory during the coming year.

There were two sets of books that his daughter wanted; Roy decided to buy them for her. Shortly afterward, Roy was injured at work. While recuperating, he entertained himself with the books he had purchased for this daughter.

To improve his spiritual life, Roy decided to fast periodically. He was pleasantly surprised when this procedure helped him keep his weight down. In past years, Roy would need a new wardrobe, due to his ever-expanding waistline.

Acceding to his daughter's wishes, once again, he allowed her to acquire a kitten. What fringe benefit did he derive form this concession? For one thing, his yard was finally safe from gophers!

Roy believes that the "happy return" theory is reasonably true. He has decided to incorporate the theory on a permanent basis.

Bread on the Water

Lou had been looking forward to receiving his income tax refund. He expected about five hundred dollars. Lou planned to take his family on a small vacation.

When the refund came, Lou's wife made a counteroffer. She and her friend would like to form a business partnership with the money. Lou, seeing his vacation slip away, reluctantly agreed.

That year, Lou broke even on his income tax, and a vacation looked out of the question again. Enter Lou's wife.

"Honey, guess what? Our business is doing real well, and during the past year, I've managed to save three thousand dollars. How would you like to go to Hawaii this summer?"

Southland Snowflakes

The weatherman had no time to warn ya'
for snow is rare in Southern California.
This day, Mr. Winter's breezes
brought something more than sneezes.

White flakes coming out of the sky
gave evidence of the Creator on high.
Flurries of snow, descending in January;
our yard was an open-air sanctuary.

Cloud's prisoners were given release
our Father aims to please.
Children, mouths open, heads back,
snow shooting toward them like flak.

Enjoy each inch with a breathless sigh
for you won't see a bit in July.
Snowmen living in front of homes,
constructed by playful gnomes.

Go into the garage, get your sled,

and let a word or two of thanks be said.

The gift that is brought by the frost—

memories won't let it be lost.

It will melt and soak into the sod;

next spring's water supply, placed by God.

Line up, hand in hand, in a row,

and thank the good Lord for some snow.

A Friend in Need

Curt was coloring Easter eggs with his family. Curt wasn't really enjoying the activity for he was preoccupied. Curt had a deep desire to become a writer. He was lacking one thing, however—a typewriter.

Curt and his family were pinched for money. They had allowed two needy friends to move in with them and two years of extra expenses had been a financial strain. There certainly was not enough money for a typewriter. Although Curt's friends were now on their own, financial recovery was slow.

Curt was brought back to the present by the doorbell. It was Barbara and Wendy, the friends with whom Curt and his family had shared their home. They had stopped by to bring Easter cards and gifts. The five people loved to exchange cards and small gifts on every holiday and birthday. Curt opened his gift; it was a small box containing a typewriter ribbon. Curt couldn't understand why the girls would give him a typewriter ribbon when he didn't have a typewriter.

After Curt had thanked the girls for the gift, they asked him to go outside. It seems they were having trouble with the trunk of their car; it would not open. Curt asked for their key and inserted it. The trunk immediately popped open, revealing a brand-new electric typewriter.

Bomb Scare!

Matt received the notice in the mail. The next day, there would be a bloodmobile at the local fire station. Matt knew that his blood type was rare and decided to be a donor.

The following day, Matt had an unusually hard day at work and was in some pain. He also had a lot of unexpected errands and chores to perform. He had all but decided to skip the blood donation, but his car seemed to point him in the direction of the fire station.

As Matt was filling out the usual forms, an announcement was made over the loudspeaker. A call had been received; someone said they had planted a bomb at the fire station and anyone who wanted to leave could do so freely. Something made Matt stay and continue with his donation. Later, Matt found out that the bomb was just a hoax.

That evening, Mark heard a sickening crash. Without warning, he had been involved in a collision. The attendants rushed him to the hospital; an immediate transfusion would be necessary. Fortunately for Mark, his rare blood had been received that very afternoon. Mark survived.

About five years later, Matt was admiring the clear nighttime sky. He decided to go for a ride in his small plane. Now, up in the air, Matt took in the panoramic view. Suddenly, he felt a pain in the area of his heart. He blacked out, and his small craft crashed in the harbor.

The Coast Guard harbor patrol rushed to the scene of the wreckage. Matt was rushed to the hospital in a state of unconsciousness. He needed an immediate transfusion to save his life. Matt's rare blood type bad been received by the blood bank the day before. The donor was named Mark.

Rain

Some people let the rain

become a reason to complain.

What would happen if the cloud

were simply not allowed?

Why treat those blessed drops

like some monstrous Cyclops?

'Tis meant to awe and inspire

and put out a raging fire.

Dry land for all critters

is a reason for the jitters.

Where you hear the thunder sound,

plants and wildlife are abound.

Rain penetrating the earth

will give us all rebirth.

Rain falling on the sod

is a blessing from God.

No need to fume and fret,

just because you hair got wet.

No need to shake your fist

because of a little mist.

Don't let a little drizzle

make you seethe and sizzle.

It's foolish to sulk and pout

when water's filling your spout.

Have you ever fought a bout

with arid land and drought?

You're not really in a jam

while there's water in your dam.

Without an occasional cloudburst,

we would surely die of thirst.

But a nice cool glass of water

doesn't even cost a quarter.

An important source of power

is generated by shower.

Without its aftermath,

You couldn't take a bath.

Although the streaks of lightning

can be a trifle frightening,

don't let a clap of thunder

cause you to go asunder.

Don't let a wet downpour

make you mad or sore.

Don't think that only sun

is the way to have your fun.

The sun may be nice and warm

but not as beautiful as a storm.

If it weren't for Noah's ark,

the world would now be dark

Won't you tell me what's the matter

with a pitter and a patter?

A little bit of hail

never sent someone to jail.

Go and tell all your kin

that a drop of rain's no sin.

I would say precipitation

is just cause for celebration!

Jack and Jill

"Argh!" Jack uttered involuntarily.

The two-ton weight of the vehicle on his chest was unbearable.

"How could the bumper jack have slipped? Why did I insist on fixing my own vehicle? Worst of all, why did I steal the tools? Oh God! Please help me."

The still-conscious man heard the back door slam.

"Jack, I heard a loud noise. What hap—?"

It was Jill.

In a display of superhuman strength, the little lady lifted the pressure from her husband's torso. He quickly but painfully scooted to safety.

"Thank you," he whispered to his lady and to his Lord.

Debt Free

How often have you heard some say, "I don't owe nobody nothing"?

While the grammar may vary (hopefully for the better), remarks like this are quite common in everyday conversation.

People who make these remarks have short memories. All of us owe all who we are and have to many people. We are indebted to all who have lived before us.

We should give credit to parents, teachers, employers, relatives, and friends who have given us direct or indirect support. Support comes in several forms—physical, mental, financial, and spiritual. Even if we choose to ignore three of the types, only a true atheist would deny the spiritual support we receive every day from a loving Creator.

The Visit

I was in the den with a book, recovering from foot surgery. I had been feeling rather discouraged. There had been a series of a couple of dozen operations over a twenty-year span, and I wondered when it would all end.

The sound of the doorbell jostled me out of my doldrums. I was pleasantly surprised to see our minister of outreach and one of his younger visitation volunteers. I was particularly surprised by the presence of the younger man. We had been in the same Sunday school class several years earlier, and I knew him to be very quiet and shy. These two attributes do not usually correlate well with visitations.

The minister of outreach dominated most of the conversation, and after about twenty minutes, he and his assistant (along with my wife and I) joined hands has the minister gave a beautify prayer for speedy recovery.

Later that afternoon, I went to the doctor to have my stitches removed. The doctor told me that I had never before healed so quickly and that I would be able to return to work a week earlier that we had anticipated.

The next day, I called the younger visitor and thanked him for taking time out from his family to visit me. He told me that was the first visit he had ever made and thanked me for my words of encouragement.

I am thankful to be part of the body of Christ, and I am thankful for all the other parts of the body. Whatever our position, we all need encouragement, and we should all offer one another encouragement in return. To us the words of Jesus, "Freely ye have received, freely give" (Matt. 10:8).

Marie

About six months ago, I started noticing a lady who attended our church in a wheelchair.

Some months after her first appearance, after the sermon, our pastor invited anyone who felt moved to come to the altar for prayer or healing.

I saw Marie, the lady in the wheelchair, make her approach to the altar (aided by her husband); I felt in my heart that she would be healed. I expected her to leap out of her wheelchair after the elders laid hands on her and prayed. To my utter disappointment and shock, no such thing happened. I spent much time in prayer about the matter.

About a month later, Marie appeared again at the altar with the same disappointing results. I somehow couldn't accept this. A month later, when she came forward a third time, I was moved by her faith and went to the altar myself to add my prayers to those of our leaders.

When we were done praying, I asked her if she would like to get up out of her wheelchair (fully believing she was healed). I came to find out later that she was almost deaf, in addition to her other problem. Still, I kept on praying for her and asked others in our church to do the same. Even my junior high school students joined in.

A few weeks later, just before Sunday school began, Marie came into our classroom still in her wheelchair. But I instantly sensed something different about her. She told me her hearing had improved to almost normal (which I quickly verified by our conversation). She also told me that she had gotten out of her wheelchair several times at home for some preliminary walking exercises.

We would all like instant miracles, but many times, we experience more gradual miracles. Sometimes, they are so gradual, they go almost unnoticed.

After hearing her report, I immediately remembered the story about the persevering lady who was finally helped by the corrupt judge "because she was not ashamed to keep on asking."

So if your hopes and dreams still seem unattainable, remember the words of Jesus and "keep on asking"!

Divine Intercession

When an area averages ten inches of rainfall per year, it is categorized as semidesert. Much of the acreage in California falls into this category. Since California leads the nation in number of inhabitants, water is precious.

After heavy rains in 1969, many people living in the foothills complained of flooding. Within seven years, however, many reservoirs were dangerously low. Water was being rationed in some areas, and many crops failed due to the prolonged drought. Many people stopped watering their lawns, and many others quit washing their cars.

Two consecutive years of above-average rainy seasons have brought the reservoirs up to normal levels. However, it would take another heavy rainy season the following year to replenish the water table.

Some of the people have given thanks for this important source of life. How about you?

Fire

It began as an ordinary autumn in Southern California. In November, a brush fire began in the San Gabriel Mountains. Brush fires are quite common in the autumn in Southern California. That particular fire was magnified by prevailing winds known as "Santa Anas."

The winds whipped this fire completely out of control. After a week, the fire still burned. Chemicals were dropped from helicopters, while two hundred professional firefighters battled the flames from the ground.

On the eighth day, the fire was threatening many homes in the foothills. On Thanksgiving morning, with twenty minutes of gentle rain, God accomplished what men and technology could not achieve. He extinguished the fire.

Ben and Betty had planned to go to Las Vegas for a four-day weekend. The possibility of having to evacuate their home made the couple decide to stay home. That evening, with their home safe from fire, Ben and Betty were preparing Thanksgiving dinner for their guests. As Ben was carving, he called to his wife, "Come on, honey. Get the kids, and let's offer a prayer of thanks."

Betty surprised her husband when she answered, "What have I go to be thankful for? I could have been living it up in Las Vegas if it weren't for that stupid old fire."

Harbors of Arbor

In cities, they muffle sounds,

provide wood for merry-go-rounds.

In suburbs, they filter the air,

provide fruit when you're hungry as a bear.

Their beauty is solid, not sheer;

leaves release moisture into our atmosphere.

When Mr. Sun's heat does invade,

our friend good ol' tree gives us shade

Branches are havens for birds,

give us enjoyment without words.

Whether in woods or in bogs,

cute critters like hollowed-out logs.

Trees are truly essential;

they keep rains from becoming torrential.

So let us get down on our knees

to thank our Creator for trees.

Body of Christ

Are Christians Always Right?

There is a subtle pitfall in being a Christian. If we continually equate Christianity with perfection, there is the danger that we will reach the conclusion that we can do no wrong.

This way of thinking will affect our relationships and our behavior toward others. It will also be a determining factor in our relationship with God. To be a Christian means to be a follower of Jesus Christ. The Bible itself proves that followers can stray.

Ananias and his wife were financially contributing members of the early church, and yet they were also liars.

Judas Iscariot followed Jesus for three years. What were his motives? If Judas had really understood and believed in Jesus, could he have become the ultimate traitor?

As the saying goes, "we are not perfect—we are forgiven," should this fill us with pride? No! It should fill us with a spirit of humility and an attitude of mercy toward everyone (both Christians and non-Christians).

This is the Spirit and attitude that motivates Jesus.

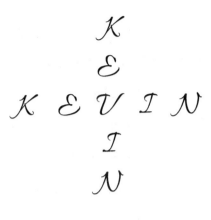

The letters in the title form a plus sign because this young man has been a plus factor in my life. About a year ago, the young people in our church went to a youth convention in Seattle. While most were able to attend the convention, a few were left behind. I had just been appointed Sunday school teacher for the junior high department. I was concerned about those unable to attend the convention, so I arranged to take them for an afternoon of miniature golfing on a Saturday.

I arose at three in the morning, for I have to work on Saturdays. After work, I made the thirty-mile trip to my house. First, I spruced up the car, and then I did likewise to myself. I made the fifteen-mile drive to church but arrived to find an empty parking lot.

I was just about to turn around for home, when I noticed Kevin sitting on the far wall. We waited together for a while so that no latecomers would be left behind. My only charge and I had a thoroughly enjoyable afternoon together, and then I drove him home.

I had accepted the position of Sunday school teacher, only on a tentative basis; that evening, I decided to accept a permanent appointment. If Kevin had not showed up, I might have made a different decision.

Kevin will always have a special place in my heart and in my prayers. Recently, he presented me with a beautiful desk set; he had made it in his woodshop class. I will always treasure it, along with the friendship of K-E-V-I-N.

Kind
Efficient
Virtuous
Incorruptible
Needed

Still Glad

Last Sunday, while ushering, a woman's faith made a permanent impression within me. The congregation was singing a hymn, when I noticed a latecomer in the vestibule. Before the glass door to the sanctuary was even opened, this grand lady was already singing . . . loudly and clearly.

What filled her with such devotion? Did she have more to be thankful for than the rest of us had? I hardly think so. She was in a wheelchair; she was paralyzed from the neck down.

She Saw the Light

When ushering for any of our worship services, it is my custom to walk up and down the aisles to ensure that everyone in attendance has received a worship bulletin.

Last Sunday, while engaging in my usual practice, I noticed an unaccompanied elderly woman without a printed guide. I approached the lady and asked her if she would like a service bulletin. The dear lady told me that she had no use for one because she could not see.

I have no way of knowing to what degree the sightless lady benefited by her attendance. But by her presence, I received an extra blessing.

God's Will

Will developed a problem with the cornea of his eye during his middle years. Despite expert treatment, the cornea gradually deteriorated. Though he was now fifty-eight years old, and it had been five years since his last attempt to have his eye repaired, Will never quite gave up hope.

Caught in the vise of the energy crunch, Will started looking around for someone with whom to carpool. This was not an easy task for Will; he was quiet and shy.

One day, while reporting for work, a man two dozen years his junior asked Will where he lived. Upon hearing Will's reply, Jack told Will they lived only two miles apart. This was no ordinary carpool; both men lived about thirty miles from work and had to report at 4:00 a.m., Tuesday through Saturday.

From the beginning, Jack could sense Will's reticence to open up. It wasn't until they had been driving together for six months that Will mentioned his corneal difficulty.

The next day, while Jack was sorting mail, he felt a pull at the back of his long hair. The playful hand belonged to Paul; the men had not seen each other in two years. Since they were on company time, the reunion lasted less than a minute.

When Paul left, Jack remembered that five or ten years earlier, Paul was involved with the Lions Club eye bank project. Upon remembering this, Jack looked for Paul on his lunch hour.

Now able to talk more freely, Jack learned that Paul had hurt himself the day before while doing some heavy lifting. For this reason, Paul had been sent to the main office to see a safety film on proper lifting techniques.

Jack now took the opportunity to mention his carpool partner's problem to Paul. It so happened that Paul was now chairman of the board for the Lions Club and was still very much involved with the eye bank project.

Together, the two men set out to find Will. After introductions were exchanged, Jack turned Will's problem over to Paul and went back to work.

On the way home from work, Will told Jack that Paul would set him up with a cornea transplant.

Utilizing the good news, Jack told Will the full story of how God had used the circumstances of three people to restore Will's physical sight and to renew his spiritual sight.

Jesus and Elvis

While many may be shocked at the linking together of these two famous names, there is really no need to be shocked.

Financially deprived childhoods did not keep either of these two from gathering a large following. Both names contain five letters. Both men dominated their earthly eras. Not many men are known all over the world by only their first name—Jesus and Elvis are two of them.

Elvis Presley believed in Jesus (God). While many people scorned Elvis because of his stage mannerisms, he never failed to inspire me with his renditions of spiritual songs.

Jesus is responsible for the sale of the most books (the Bible). Elvis is responsible for the most record sales. Both personalities devoted much of their time to helping others.

Oh yes, they have one more thing in common: through both have experienced death, they both live.

Does God Need Us?

Recently, a coworker began a conversation with me with the following statement: "Why does God need us?"

Surprised, I replied, "He doesn't."

She then asked me why we are told to worship Him with all our hearts, minds, souls, and strength if He doesn't need our worship.

I gave her the following illustration as my answer: I told her that after my wife and I got married, we didn't *need* a child; we *wanted* someone with whom to share our life. With God's help, we created this new life.

Our child *needs* us and depends on us for continued life, knowledge, etc. In the same manner, God wanted to share a beautiful universe with us forever. He did this not because He needs us. But if we *want* to receive His gift of eternal life and love, we *need* Him.

Mavericks

Over the years, throughout the world, Christianity has been perceived incorrectly by many. Even among Christians, there have been some incorrect perceptions. All Christians do not feel obligated to obey man-made opinions given by some remote religious leader; nothing could be further from the truth.

The Christian values individuality and is an independent thinker. Many do not believe in or follow Jesus Christ until they have examined all the evidence thoroughly. God manifests His will in different ways to different people.

Jesus Christ was not bound by tradition. Whenever religious traditions conflicted with God's will for Him, Jesus followed God's will. How was Jesus so in tune with God's will? He spent much time in prayer; He had a thorough knowledge of the Bible (God's words). Jesus also had the ability to elevate his mind from worldly cares by fasting.

So then, while the secular world blares out in favor of conformity, the Christian is really a nonconformist.

A Breath of Fresh Air

Carl was in the construction business; he installed what is called drywall. Lately, Carl had become quite concerned with his state of health. Carl's lungs had deteriorated due to the contents in the drywall. Carl's doctor advised him to get out of his trade in order to save his lungs.

Carl wanted to open a Christian bookstore but lacked the necessary experience. One day, Carl's friend Warren received an offer to manage a Christian bookstore. Warren didn't really feel that he would be a suitable manager, for various reasons. Warren, remembering Carl's condition, recommended him for the position. Carl gratefully *lunged* at the opportunity.

After several years of experience as manager, Carl felt that he was ready to open his own store. He opened it with the blessings of his former boss. Carl feels that he received help when he needed it. Carl hopes that the books he sells will give his brethren help and inspiration when they need it.

Because She Cared

Todd's background had given him a totally negative concept of God. He pictured God following him around, zapping him for every mistake and every error of omission. For this reason, Todd had avoided going to church for many years; the sermons only made him nervous.

At his wife's suggestion, Todd decided to give her Sunday school class a try. The open discussions and wide variety of opinions were right up Todd's alley. During one class, the subject of the Bible cropped up.

Many of the people in attendance voiced their opinions on the validity and worthiness of the ancient Book. Todd had tried reading the Bible several times but could never seem to understand or enjoy it. He decided to relate his experience to the group. He fully expected to be the object of condescension and ridicule. Instead, many of the members actually commended him for his honesty; Todd was impressed.

As he was leaving the church that morning, Todd heard a pair of high heels running toward his direction. The owner of the shoes was Janet, one of his Sunday school classmates.

"Todd, I heard what you said in class this morning, about your difficulty in understanding the Bible. I would like to give you this modern translation. I think you'll find it much easier to understand than what you've been reading."

Todd thanked the lady for her concern and drove home.

Upon arriving, Todd put the Bible in a drawer and promptly forgot about it. Several years later, Todd was straightening out some cluttered drawers. He came across the Bible Janet had given him. He opened it and began to read the New Testament.

He couldn't believe his eyes. "This can't be the Bible!" he exclaimed. "I can understand it."

After a thorough reading, Todd decided to be baptized again and to commit his life to the God of love whom he had now come to know.

Within a year, Todd was serving as an usher and Sunday school teacher . . . because she cared!

God's Toolbox

God set out for work this morning. He had a lot of lives to repair. He used all His well-known tools to accomplish most of the tasks.

He used Henry Hammer to drive home a point. He utilized Willie Wrench to loosen someone's firm grip on destruction. Next, God used Sammy Screwdriver to tighten up a few loose morals. Peter Pliers was used to bend some ways of thinking. Harry Handsaw was used to bring people to the right measure of humility.

While all this was happening, Keith Keyhole Saw and Carl Crowbar were lying unused at the bottom of the box.

They complained to each other loudly. "When will God use us?" they wailed.

Knowing the tools were waiting to be used, the Lord had a pleasant surprise for them both.

Late that afternoon, Carl Crowbar was used to pry open a bunch of closed minds, and Keith Keyhole Saw was utilized to go into an area that none of the other tools could reach. Before the day was finished, God had used them all.

Division!

Much has been said about division in the church; non-Christians point with pride and use it as a reason for not believing. I would like to share with you a story from the book of Acts. It is the story of the relationship between the apostle Paul and Barnabas.

Much has been written about Paul, and he is renowned. Barnabas, although not as well known as Paul, is a fine Christian also.

And so it was that Joseph, a Levite born in Cypress, whom the apostles called Barnabas (which means "one who encourages") sold a field he owned, brought the money, and turned it over to the apostles (Acts 4:36–37).

Paul went to Jerusalem and tried to join the disciples. But they would not believe that he was a disciple, and they were all afraid of him. Then Barnabas came to his aid and took him to the apostles. He explained to them how Paul had preached in the name of Jesus in Damascus (Acts 9:26–27).

The news about this reached the church in Jerusalem, so they sent Barnabas to Antioch. When he arrived and saw how God had blessed the people, he was glad and urged them all to be faithful and true to the Lord with all their hearts. Barnabas was a good man, full of the Holy Spirit and faith, and many people were brought to the Lord (Acts 11:22–25).

In the church at Antioch, there were some prophets and teachers: Barnabas, Simeon (called the black), Lucius (from Cyrene), Manaen (who had been brought up with Governor Herod), and Paul. While they were serving the Lord and fasting, the Holy Spirit said to them, "Set apart for me Barnabas and Paul, to do the work to which I have called them." They fasted and prayed, placed their hands on them, and sent them off (Acts 13:1–3).

After the people had left the meeting, Paul and Barnabas were followed by many Jews and by many gentiles who had been converted to Judaism. The apostles spoke to them and encouraged them to keep on living in the grace of God (Acts 13:43).

When Barnabas and Paul heard what they were about to do, they tore their clothes and ran into the middle of the crowd, shouting, "Why are you doing this? We ourselves are only human beings like you! We are here to announce the Good News, to turn you away from these worthless things to the living God, who made heaven, earth, sea, and all that is in them.

"In the past, He allowed all people to go their own ways. But He has always given evidence of His existence by the good things He does. He gives you rain from heaven and crops at the right times. He gives you food and fills your hearts with happiness."

Even with these words, the apostles could hardly keep the crowd from offering sacrifice to them (Act 14:14–18).

The whole group was silent as they heard Barnabas and Paul report all the miracles and wonders that God had performed through them among the gentiles (Acts 15:12).

Paul and Barnabas spent some time in Antioch, and together with many others, they taught and preached the word of the Lord (Acts 15:35).

Barnabas wanted to take John Mark with them, but Paul did not think it was right to take him because he had not stayed with them to the end of their mission and had turned back and left them in Pamphylia. There was a sharp argument, and they separated. Barnabas took Mark and sailed off for Cyprus, while Paul chose Silas and left, commended by the believers to the care of the Lord's grace (Acts 15:37–40).

It is difficult to think the separation was permanent; for later, in the New Testament, Paul refers to Mark as "my son in the Lord."

As for all the different church denominations, I like to think of them as different roads leading to the same place.

Christianity Is Freedom

Some people have gotten the idea that to be a Christian is to be cast into a mold of conformity or to be standardized into dullness. Some feel that to commit their lives to Jesus is to be robbed of their individuality. Nothing could be further from the truth.

God made each of us a little different from each other. In the book of John, we are told that the Word of God created the world (John 1:3). If the Word of God was powerful enough to create the world, is it not powerful enough to sustain us through this trail toward eternal life?

The Bible tells us to be transformed by the renewing of our minds (Rom. 12:2). Since the Bible is God's written word, then reading it gives us the power to be renewed and transformed.

Renewal and transformation are the opposites of conformity and standardization. Sometimes, we feel we would stand a better chance of gaining salvation if we could be like this person or that person. Again, we gain encouragement from the Bible (God's word); each servant is able to succeed because God is able to make him succeed (Rom. 14:4).

Let's all thank God for success in our own right.

Help

A few Sundays ago, while ushering at the morning service, the minister of outreach called me aside and asked me to deliver a message for him.

My mission took me to the choir loft. Upon delivering the message, I started back down the stairs. As I touched the first step, I stumbled and would have fallen down; but at the very moment, one of the men in the choir saw me and extended his hand for a handshake.

It was quite a coincidence that he was grasping my hand just when I stumbled. Had we not reached out to each other, I surely would have taken a tumble.

After reflecting upon this incident, I concluded that there are times in our spiritual lives when we are ready to slip and fall. Perhaps if we surround ourselves with Christian friends, the chances of falling would be minimized.

The Maundy Thursday Experience

On the night before Good Friday, it is customary for the members of our church to gather together for prayer, communion, foot washing, and spiritual sharing. I had wanted to attend one of these services for some time, but because of my schedule, I had never been able to participate. Last year, my wish came true, and I was able to attend. I would like to share the experience with all of you.

A sign outside the door requested silence. My daughter, her friend, and I took the first three vacant seats. The room was lit only by candles.

When everyone was seated, our pastor asked me to offer a communion prayer. Although I was unprepared, the words came. I expressed our gratitude for the opportunity to meet freely and openly to commemorate Jesus's last night with His apostles. We accepted Christ's body and blood from gold trays in remembrance of Him.

Following Communion, the women entered another room, leaving an all-male group in our room. Half of us got up, girded ourselves with a linen towel, and filled basins with water. I looked forward to washing the feet of a good friend who had retired form his profession several years earlier; the spiritual feeling between us was warm and radiant. However, when one of our leading ushers came to wash my feet, I felt slightly uncomfortable and unworthy; but I did not protest as did the apostle Peter.

After putting things back in order, we gathered in a circle, and each of us took turns telling what Jesus Christ had meant in his life. It was wonderful to hear grown men (and one not so grown) unashamedly give their own unique testimony of our Lord. Although everyone had something meaningful and interesting to say, the man I most remember is the one who said the least.

He was an elderly man; his hair was as white as freshly fallen snow. When he spoke of our Lord, his eyes became misty with gratitude and reverence. Through his misty eyes, he seemed to see the Prince of peace.

I can't remember a word he said, but I hope I can grow as close to our Creator as that white-haired gentleman was on Maundy Thursday.

Hand and Foot

Although Hand and Foot belong to the same body, they despise each other. Neither of them ever misses an opportunity to point out the other's shortcomings.

Hand dislikes foot because it was very difficult for foot to grasp things. Foot despises hand because hand never took him anywhere. Hand figures foot can't be important because foot can't salute or wave goodbye. Foot knows hand can't bear as much pressure as he bore; why, Hand doesn't even own a shoe!

One day, hand and foot had to work together in order to win a game of tug-of-war. When the game was over, each admitted that the victory would have been impossible without the other's assistance. The game resulted in a healthy mutual respect.

Cheating, Lying & Stealing

Vexing Vandals

Bill and Carol had worked in Bill's father's business since they were married. It was a small family business, and the young couple bought it upon Ted's retirement. Bill and his wife had to borrow a considerable amount of money in order to become the new owners. Their water gardens specialized in growing and marketing water lilies. They also sold pond accessories, and they also serviced ponds.

On Saturday night, three young men decided to have some fun. They climbed over a fence and proceeded to vandalize a water garden.

When Bill and Carol came to open for business on Monday morning, they stood aghast. The sight of dozens of rare fish lying dead in the driveway was a shock; the stench will not be soon forgotten. When all the damage had been tabulated, the loss had reached the seven-thousand-dollar mark.

Bill decided to buy a trained guard dog to prevent any future destruction. The dog he chose as not an ordinary one. The price tag on the animal was over a thousand dollars. The dog had spent over six months in specialized training.

Upon a code word, given only by its owner, the pet would be instantly transformed into a killer. He was taught not to ever bark so that his location could not be detected. He was trained to stay at least six feet from any fence. The dog was taught to stay hidden until its services were required.

When he attacked, limbs were ignored; he was interested only in vital organs. If more than one vandal came, the animal would wait patiently until all of them had entered the premises. He would then dispose of them very quickly, beginning with the last criminal and ending with the first.

Although the necessary signs were posted, the owners were very reluctant to employ such drastic measures; but their future was at stake.

Will anyone else attempt to vandalize their investment?

For everyone's sake, I hope not.

For the Record

Randy was happy with his life. He lived in a display case of a record store. People would come in and admire him and his friends. Randy felt especially important one day because he was number 1 on the hit record chart.

Late that afternoon, a boy came into the store. The boy grabbed Randy by the throat and took his size 45 RPM jacket off. The boy then looked around before thrusting Randy into his new zippered jacket. It was totally dark in the new jacket, and Randy was aware of being in motion.

When the boy got home, he took Randy out of his hiding place and put him in a dark closet. A few days later, the boy opened the closet and removed Randy. The light hurt Randy's eyes.

The boy put Randy in some kind of torture chamber. In the chamber, Randy would be spun around until he was dizzy. But, worse than that, he would be scratched by a needle until he cried out in pain; his cries could be heard all over the house. Randy could hear the boy saying works like "boss" and "groovy." The boy never came to his rescue in time but would take him out after the torture was all over.

After some weeks, Randy was joined in the closet by some of his former friends at the record store. His friends told Randy how their value was going to increase. Already, the manager was installing closed circuit television cameras to monitor their behavior.

One day, the boy went into the record store to buy a new album. He noticed that the prices of albums had gone up to cover the costs of security equipment and increased insurance premiums.

The boy thought, unhappily, *The manager of this store is really ripping the people off!*

Burn, Baby, Burn

Harry looked over his ledgers disconsolately. Despite all his managerial skill, his small manufacturing plant was on the verge of bankruptcy. Harry was at his wit's end. He removed the phone from the hook so that he could think without interruption.

The plant was well insured, and all the employees had already gone home. Harry hesitated just a moment. He lit the match and set fire to all he had worked so hard to build. He consoled himself with the thought that the insurance money would at least keep him out of bankruptcy; then he ran out of the smoldering building.

Harry's apartment was only a short distance away. He walked home dejectedly, entered the building, and pushed the elevator button for the twentieth floor. Upon entering the apartment, his wife greeted him and asked how things were at the plant.

Harry feigned nonchalance and asked where their little daughter was at the moment.

"Isn't she with you?" Helen asked. "She was missing you and I told her to walk over to your plant and slip quietly into one of the empty offices to play until you came and got her. I tried to call and tell you but your phone was busy."

Harry, mouth agape, turned pale and tried to retrace his steps.

As soon as he got outside, Harry could see flames and smoke leaping from his former plant. It was too late.

Crash!

It was lunchtime, and Stella felt like having some tacos. It was about a hundred degrees outside, and the fifteen-year-old girl did not look forward to the half-mile walk to the store.

Her older sister had borrowed a car from one of her friends. The car was parked in the driveway, with the key in the ignition. Because of the temperature and the short distance to the store, the hungry girl decided it would be all right to use the car.

On her way back home, as she turned a corner, a bug flew into her eye. The next instant, she felt a jolt and heard the crunch of metal against metal. A man came running out of his house to survey the damage to his parked car.

Stella's parents are now six hundred dollars poorer, and the unfortunate girl is left wishing she had ridden her bicycle instead of the "borrowed" car.

Jolted by Justice

Gary was an apartment manager. The complex that he managed consisted of forty units. As Gary looked over the rent ledger, his eyes stopped on line 34. The tenant in apartment 34 had been somewhat troublesome, lately; in addition to causing trouble, he had not paid his rent for quite some time.

Gary decided to go over and talk to the tenant. After receiving no response at the door, Gary decided that Mr. George must be out. There had been quite a bit of activity around apartment 34 earlier that morning. Gary suspected that Mr. George might be skipping out without paying his back rent. Gary was glad that his property management corporation had lawyers to handle such matters. The manager returned to his office and put away his books; there was some shopping to be done.

While driving along a main thoroughfare on his return trip from the store, Gary noticed a pickup truck amidst the oncoming traffic. The speed limit was forty miles per hour on that avenue. The driver of the pickup truck, without bothering to slow down, turned into a tract of homes. He took the corner much too fast, and the refrigerator that he was hauling jumped out of the truck as though it had been shot out of a huge cannon.

When it landed, the crash could be heard a block away. The door was ripped from its hinges and sent flying; all the food was scattered. There was broken glass and food remnants strewn for half a block.

Mr. George got out of his truck and started jumping up and down in a rage. His naturally red complexion turned purple. He tried to pull at his hair, but that was difficult since he wore it in a crew-cut.

Parked across the street, Gary thought of crossing over and trying to help Mr. George salvage something but thought it best to stay away since Mr. George was irrational at the moment.

Gary continued home and put out the sign "Apartment for Rent."

The Party

Bob picked up the ringing telephone; he couldn't believe it! Bob's best friend Ron was on the line. Ron was home on weekend leave from the air force.

Ron wanted Bob to throw a party for him. This, Bob wanted to do more than anything. There was one problem—Bob had to work at the restaurant that evening. In a quandary, Bob called all his friends, including Mary, Bob's girlfriend.

Mary told Bob that, on such short notice, she would have to let him know later that evening.

After making all the arrangements, Bob called his boss at the restaurant. Bob told Stan that he had gotten food poisoning and would not be able to work that night.

After listening to the story, Stan replied: "Mary, your girlfriend, called and said to tell you she can't come to your party tonight."

There was an awkward silence, and then Stan laughed. "Go ahead and have a good time, Bob. I'll see you tomorrow."

Somehow, Bob didn't have such a good time at the party.

Only the Strong Survive?

Billy and Bobby were on their way to the store; they were going to buy candy bars.

Tom, who lived down the block, rushed up to them. "Hey, how about you guys lending me some money?"

Not wanting to forfeit their afterschool treats, the boys replied, "Sorry, we don't have any money to loan you."

After purchasing their candy bars, they ran into Tom again. Noticing their half-eaten bars, Tom accused, "You guys told lies. Your souls are filled with sin."

The twosome arrived home feeling slightly guilty.

The next day, while walking home from school, the two boys spotted Tom fighting. He was beating up a smaller boy.

They heard the kid crying, "That was the only money I had! Why did you have to take it?"

Tom laughed, "Tough luck, dude. 'Only the strong survive.'"

Bobby and Billy were thinking the same thing: *I wonder how Tom's soul will survive?*

The Pen That Lied

It has been said the "figures don't lie, but liars figure." The following story will illustrate the ramifications:

A supervisory position became vacant, upon the retirement of a company stalwart. This particular company prided itself on its high production, and everything was geared to meet these goals. In an effort to fill the void created by the supervisor's departure, several aspirants were given trial periods.

The competition between each production group was stiff. With this thought in mind, one of the aspiring supervisors began falsifying production reports. Since Pat's work crews always seemed to have the highest productivity level—on paper, that is—our figure juggler received the much-hoped-for promotion.

Unfortunately for Pat, the future holds a potential demotion. Deceptive skill cannot be used to pen a name into the Book of the Living; a Boss will be faced whom no one can fool.

Father Knows Bess

Clark and his father lived alone since the death of Clark's mother. The boy's father realized that his son sorely missed having a mother. From time to time, he would bring the boy to his sister Bess's house. Clark loved his Aunt Bess and her son, Johnny.

One summer, when Clark was about nine, he was invited to stay a week at the home of his favorite relatives. The boy had spent much of the summer collecting baseball cards; he lacked only several dozen to complete the entire set.

During the course of the week, Johnny showed Clark his baseball card collection. Johnny also had almost the entire set; he also had dozens of doubles. As Clark looked through Johnny's doubles, he found about a dozen that he needed to complete his set. However, Johnny explained that he was saving the doubles, in hopes of making trades for the ones he lacked.

The night before Clark was to go back home, he was overcome by covetousness. He snuck into Johnny's room, removed the prized cards, and hid them in his suitcase. Clark didn't sleep well that night.

The following morning, as the three relatives awaited the arrival of Clark's father, Johnny spoke to Clark, "I wanted to give you the cards you need to complete your set. But when I looked in my collection box, I couldn't find them. I'm sorry."

Clark ran into the guest room, dug out the stolen cards, and gave them to his cousin. "I'm the one who's sorry. I don't know why I took them from you. I just wanted them so badly. Please ask Aunt Bess not to mention it to my father. It would really hurt him to hear that his son is a thief!"

"It's all right, Clark. I understand and I promise not to tell anyone."

"Thanks, Johnny. I promise never to steal anything ever again."

The Promise

Gary took great pride in his good grades at school. He did well in all subjects. But when Gary missed two months of school because of ear surgery, he started having trouble in math when he returned. To make matters worse, he had to change schools in the middle of the year.

In the new school, his classmates were further ahead in math than he was at his former school. Gary was really falling behind, and an important test was coming up. On test day, Gary sat next to the class math whiz.

It was wrong to copy someone else's work, but Gary thought, *Just this once, in order to get off the hook, until I can catch up.*

When the results were returned, Gary had received 100 percent on his math paper. Gary showed the test to his father that night after dinner. His father had trouble with math when he was in school. Gary was asked to teach his father how to answer the test questions.

When Gary was unable to show his father how to accomplish the work, his father asked Gary how he could possibly have scored 100 percent. Gary cried and admitted the truth. His father made him promise never to copy again.

Upon graduation from college, with honors, Gary was glad he had kept the promise.

Criticism

Who Is Worthy?

Justin and Sylvester were having a discussion about who was truly worthy of eternal life.

"How about Moses?" asked Justin.

"What! That murderer?" Sylvester lashed out.

"What about Peter?"

"Oh, he was too impulsive and wishy-washy" Sylvester explained.

"Then how about mighty David?" Justin ventured.

"Didn't you know that he once committed adultery?" Sylvester said with raised eyebrows.

"Well, Noah was righteous. Surely, he qualifies."

"I'm afraid not." Sylvester smirked. "He was found in a state of intoxication and nudity."

"I've got it!" Justin brightened. "The brothers James and John."

"But they once threatened to do violence," Sylvester retorted.

"Then what about Paul?" Justin pleaded.

"Paul actually took part in acts of violence when he was young," Sylvester reprimanded.

"Well then," Justin sighed in desperation, "Jesus! What's wrong with Him?"

"I can't think of anything at the moment." Sylvester frowned. "But maybe I'll think of something later."

"If anybody can do it, you can, Sylvester," marveled Justin.

Biblical Bad Guys

For some time, I have been giving much thought to some of the biblical characters traditionally displayed as "bad guys"; they have been labeled bad, as compared to us good guys (and good girls).

The Rich Young Ruler

As Jesus was starting on his way again, a man ran up, knelt before him, and asked Him, "Good Teacher, what must I do to receive eternal life?"

"Why do you call me good?" Jesus asked him. "No one is good except God alone. You know the commandments: 'Do not commit murder, do not commit adultery, do not steal, do not accuse anyone falsely, do not cheat, respect your father and your mother.'"

"Teacher," the man said, "ever since I was young, I have obeyed all these commandments."

Jesus looked straight at him *with love* and said, "If you want to be *perfect*, go and sell *all* you have and give the money to the poor, and you will have riches in heaven. Then come follow me."

When the young man heard this, he went away sad because he was very rich.

Jesus looked around at his disciples and said to them, "How hard it will be for rich people to enter the kingdom of God."

The disciples were shocked at these words, but Jesus went on to say, "My children, how hard it is to enter the kingdom of God. It is much harder for a rich person to enter the kingdom of God than for a camel to go through the eye of a needle."

When the disciples heard this, they were completely amazed. "Who, then, can be saved?" they asked him.

Jesus looked straight at them and answered, "This is impossible for man *but not for God. Everything* is possible for God."

There are several points to take note of in this story: Jesus looked at the man with love; God does not change His mind about whom He loves. Jesus directed his statement about the "eye of the needle" to the apostles; He did not condemn the rich young man. Jesus then reminded them that with God, all things are possible; could this statement not include the potential salvation of the young ruler?

I might add that there are few of us (myself included) who would be willing to sell *everything* we own. Therefore, should we not take a more liberal attitude toward this young man? If we fail to do this, we are condemning ourselves. Remember: "Judge not, lest ye be judged" (Matt. 7:1).

I myself have sat in church wagging my head at the ruler's lack of total commitment. I hope I will never do so again.

Pontius Pilate

This is one of the most maligned men in the Bible; he has been labeled no less than a murderer. Shall we take a closer look at him . . . and possibly ourselves?

Pilate did *almost* everything in his power to set Jesus free. He pleaded and cajoled the Jews, in an effort to release him. But the people, stirred up by their religious leaders, insisted on killing the Author of life, and asked, instead, for the release of Barabbas (a murderer).

I wonder how I would have reacted if I were in Pilate's place. A crowd of angry Jews screaming at me and threatening to put me in a bad light with my superior (the emperor). Even Jesus did not condemn Pilate; instead, He said to him: "You have authority over me only because it was given to you by God. So the man who handed me over to you is guilty of a *worse* sin" (John 19:11).

Pointing the Finger

Jamie and Gerald first met each other in junior high school, their lives intertwined throughout their earthly lifetimes.

Jamie was a fun-loving boy and was fairly popular in school. Gerald was rather insecure; he tried to mask his insecurity with a lot of false bravado and was adept as a put-down artist. Gerald disliked Jamie from the start and never missed an opportunity to criticize him or question his motives.

Jamie always took Gerald's "kidding" good-naturedly. Jamie was a good student and was well behaved. Gerald always ridiculed Jamie for his lifestyle and tried to get others to do the same (sometimes with much success).

Gerald spent most of his time thinking of tricks to play on Jamie and of ways to make him look small. Jamie passed these tricks off with a shrug or a laugh. Jamie never tried to get even; instead, he pursued building a life for himself in a positive manner.

He was helpful and courteous to others, attended church and Sunday school, read his Bible, and tried to live by it. He even invited Gerald to Sunday school sometimes, but Gerald would turn him down and scoff at him for "wasting his time on that religious stuff."

As the two boys grew older, Jamie attended college on the G.I. Bill. After serving in the war, he opened up a successful business and was blessed with a fine family and a happy life. Gerald avoided the draft, dropped out of college, and drifted from job to job.

Whenever the two men crossed paths, Gerald would use the opportunity to try to spot some flaw in Jamie's successful way of living. Gerald never really believed Jamie was as nice as he seemed. He was dead sure that underneath, Jamie was no better than he.

Many times, he would go places with Jamie just to try to catch him doing or saying something wrong, though he never could. He persisted in his disbelief of Jamie's integrity. This disbelief gradually became an obsession to Gerald, and he devoted more and more time to finding out the real truth about Jamie.

As their lives neared the half-century mark, Jamie was struck down by an automobile and pronounced dead on arrival at the local hospital.

Gerald, upon hearing the news, told everyone, "See! I always knew there was something that didn't ring true about that guy."

Within several years, Gerald was dead too; his was a lingering and painful departure.

When Judgment Day came, Jesus asked Gerald Fain to step forward and tell what he had done with his life.

Gerald explained that he had spent most of his time trying to unmask Jamie Brooks's false façade so that others would not be taken in by his pious veneer. Gerald further explained that he was glad he had finally succeeded (referring to Jamie's untimely death).

Jesus read to Gerald form the Bible's book of Matthew, the third through the fifth verses of the seventh chapter:

> "Why do you see the speck that is in your
> brother's eye? Or how can you say to your
> brother: "Let me take the speck out of your
> eye," when there is the log in your own
> eye? You hypocrite, first take the log out of
> your own eye, and then you will see clearly
> to take the speck out of the brother's eye."

After speaking these words, Jesus sent Gerald to the outer darkness—the place where people cry and gnash their teeth.

Jesus then called Jamie Brooks forward. After reading Jamie's name from the Book of Life, Jesus told him to go and join the feast with Abraham and the other saints.

The Dummy?

Because of his limited vocabulary and his inability to express himself clearly, Tony was known to most of his fellow employees as the dummy. It was unfortunate that Tony's pinioned tongue was more easily perceived than this financial ability.

Despite a nickname that would handicap others, Tony utilized his financial acumen to snowball several wise investments into a small fortune. His success has enabled him to retire early, and he is now living quite comfortably.

Meanwhile, Tony's "intellectual superiors" are looking around for a new dummy.

Discernment

The Cover

"You can't judge a book by its cover." I found out how true these words are last week.

Several of us were doing some strenuous work. While most of us showed the strain, I noticed a young Oriental man smiling and whistling. I had to admire his cheerful cover. I said to him, "You certainly are a happy man."

"Oh, I no happy," he blurted back at me. He then proceeded to enumerate all the reasons for his unhappiness.

Many people mask their true feelings with a false façade. It is difficult to diagnose a problem when the symptoms are incongruous. Once we get past the cover, however, our senses can pick up what's inside.

Two Faces Has He

Just as God works through people, the devil has a similar ability. When a person is openly hostile or antagonistic, his position is plain to see. But what of the person who, while enjoying his deceitful ways, smiles and nods approvingly? Was Eve approached with a reptile smile or a frown? Probably a smile.

So then, how do we distinguish someone's true motives? Thanks to the Holy Spirit for the gift of discernment (2 Cor. 11:14–15).

Employment

A Waitress

Although the hard floor hurts my feet,

I will escort you to your seat.

Even though my car broke down,

I won't grimace nor give you frown.

I try to give my honest hunch

when someone asks "What's good for lunch?"

When men insist on trying to flirt,

I try to smile and not be curt.

If your children drop a glass,

I grin politely and let it pass.

I never refuse to serve your dinner,

just because you are a sinner.

When you get well done instead of rare,

I absorb the blame because I care.

I only ask one thing of you—

remember it's a restaurant . . . not a zoo.

Under the Gun

They called him Big Al, but without his gun, Al wasn't so big. Al worked at the postal sorting center. Al hated his job; but even more, he hated his supervisor, Mr. Fredericks.

After a particularly bad day, Al decided what he would do to Mr. Fredericks. Al's supervisor only asked that each employee put in a day's work for a day's pay. To Al, this was asking too much.

The following day, Al brooded as he sorted a tray of letters. Finally, he could take it no longer. Al put his hand in his pocket and headed in the direction of Mr. Fredericks. About halfway there, Al tripped over a heavy object that had not been there before, Al instinctively threw his hands out in front to break his fall.

An alert guard spotted the metal object in Al's hand; the guard grabbed Al and subdued him.

Al hasn't changed much; he hates his new job too. What is his new job? Al is engaged in the manufacture of license plates.

Each Will Be Rewarded

Ernie and Vic worked in the same building; their place of employment was about all they had in common. Vic knew the rules well; he was capable of doing more. Vic thought he may as well take advantage of the situation. Ernie was just the opposite. Although he also knew the rules, he always did as much as he could.

Vic, who always had one eye out for what was going on around him, approached Ernie. "Hey, Ernie, how come you work so hard when you could be taking it easy like me?"

Ernie thought carefully before he responded. "For the Son of Man shall come in the glory of his Father with his angels; and then he shall reward every man according to his works" (Matt. 16:27).

Vic trudged away, muttering to himself, "Now what on earth did he mean by that?"

What about You?

The office was practically empty; almost everyone had just left for lunch. A few more minutes of paperwork and George would join them.

Mr. Finlay, the office manager, sat down on the corner of George's desk. He poured himself some coffee and lit up a large cigar.

"George," he said, "I don't know how I put up with all these people."

Thus was the beginning of a twenty-minute spiel.

Mr. Finlay continued, "Casey smokes the most foul-smelling cigars. Margaret's always complaining that the office is too hot. Thelma complains that it's too cold. Helen thinks she's the boss, and Rick thinks he's Don Juan. Ralph is late about twice a week, and Barbara spends too much time in the ladies' lounge.

"Fred moves about as fast as a turtle, and Mike never wants to work overtime. Frank's always arguing with someone, and Tony's a real dummy. I smelled liquor on Bob's breath the other day, and Debbie's accuracy rate isn't very high.

"I've actually heard Chuck talk to himself, and Harry's a real grouch. Mary's a busybody, and Pat seems more concerned with her appearance than with getting any work done. I'm pretty sure Kathy is cheating on her husband, and Jerry sure calls in sick a lot."

Throughout the conversation, George attempted to complete his work and would give an acknowledging nod once in a while in an effort to be courteous.

Finally, Mr. Finlay had covered everyone. George took off his glasses, looked at Mr. Finlay, and said, "And what about you, Mr. Finlay, what did you accomplish during the past twenty minutes?"

Mr. Finaly was furious. He stormed away, muttering to himself, "Nobody around here understands me."

What! No Raise?

Cathy and Ray were typical office workers; they were bored with their jobs. After a year and a half on the job, the routine seemed to become dull. Cathy and Ray, vaguely aware of this feeling, started spending more and more time visiting with each other. They seldom saw each other outside of their work environment, but they spent much of their work time giving each other all the latest details of their (and everyone else's) lives.

Their boss, Ted, was quite puzzled. The department that Cathy and Ray were in never seemed to finish their work on time. Whenever Ted came into their office, they always seemed busy. He didn't know what went on after he left. Ted knew that Cathy and Ray were good workers when they first started, as he spent a lot of time training them in the early months of their employment.

In the office next door to Cathy and Ray's, Mel worked. Mel was a quiet sort of man, and his efficiency and devotion to duty was a source of amusement to Cathy and Ray. As the year was nearing its end, Ted was making plans to give raises to everyone in all departments.

Meanwhile, Cathy and Ray's department was falling further and further behind schedule. Something had to be done immediately. Ted had to hire additional help to take up the slack in Cathy and Ray's department.

Because of this unexpected expense, Ted was not able to give Cathy or Ray the raise they were hoping for.

When Cathy and Ray found out that Mel received a raise and they didn't, they disliked him even more. The two complained loudly to each other, "Why didn't we get a raise?"

Fracturing Fractions

Not surprisingly, many people dislike their jobs. Ideally, these people could find more suitable employment; for some, this may not be possible. Another approach would be for them to try to enjoy the job, despite their true feelings. This approach will not work for all people either.

Well then, what is left for the remainder of us? Let's put things in perspective: There are 168 hours in a week. Most of us have to spend 40 hours per week on the job—less than 25 percent.

Also, consider this: Most of us begin working when we're eighteen years old, and most retire at age sixty-five. This leaves us with seventeen years' reprieve at the begging of our lives and probably a few toward the end. When these two factors are taken into consideration, the 25 percent work time is reduced much further.

To those of you who have not yet chosen a career, I strongly advise you to seek a satisfying and enjoyable one. If you do this, you will be able to disregard the first three-quarters of this article!

A Day's Work

Mr. Daley, the kindly president of a small manufacturing firm, surveyed the situation. He noticed that the production workers had been getting done about twenty minutes early. To show his appreciation for their efforts, he let them go home early . . . with pay. This went on for several weeks, to the delight of all concerned.

One day, however, the work schedule was quite heavy.

Marilyn complained to her partner, "I'll bet we'll all have to stay until quitting time. That Mr. Daley would never let us go home early when there's work left undone."

Upon hearing the conversation, Mr. Daley made a decision. In the future, everyone would stay the full eight hours—whether or not their work was completed.

After hearing the announcement, Marilyn remarked to her partner, "See, I knew that Mr. Daley was a scrooge!"

Charity Belongs at Home

Today, I witnessed a rather common chapter in the book of human affairs: Dorothy, a woman who works in the same complex as I, paraded around on a mercenary mission.

It seems her son was entering a jogathon. The idea was for every person to pledge a specified amount in advance for every lap the boy could complete in a one-hour period.

The sight of collecting on company time is all too common. Aside from interrupting the production and trains of thought of her fellow employees, Dorothy (who is paid about seven or eight dollars per hour) used up two hours of time. Therefore, her employer unknowingly contributed about fifteen dollars to a cause unknown to him. Does this seem charitable?

Fun People

Wayne and Todd enjoyed their jobs immensely—they hardly ever did any work for they were too busy with "more important" things. There were football pools to organize, practical jokes to play, outside interests to discuss, and social relationships to extend. Any work they might accomplish was incidental.

One day, their supervisor remarked to them, "You two guys seem to have more fun that anyone here."

"It's fun because we make it fun," Todd immediately shot back.

It was Friday afternoon, and the entire crew looked forward to spending the weekend with their families; some of them had made plans. But due Wayne and Todd's antics, all the stick-in-the-muds had their days off cancelled instead.

Getting Even

Fred and Hank had a good employer-employee relationship. Occasionally, they even attended the same church.

One Friday, while Hank was looking over his pay stub, he noticed that he had been shortchanged by thirty dollars. A verse of scripture suddenly popped into his head, which he had heard in a sermon: "I thy brother offends thee, go to him and tell him his fault" (Matt. 18:15).

Casting this thought aside, Hank thought to himself, *Why quibble over thirty dollars?*

After a time, Hank found himself avoiding Fred outside of their work environment. Little by little, Hand started "borrowing" office supplies for his personal use.

While Fred was going over his quarterly business expenses, he noticed a thirty-dollar discrepancy in his books. He then traced down the deficit in Hank's paycheck. He wanted to tell Hank and apologize, but he was slightly embarrassed at this own oversight.

Besides, he thought, *someone's got to make up for all the office supplies that have been missing.*

After closing out his books, Fred locked his office, said goodbye to Hank, and drove home. Upon arriving home, Fred realized he had left his books at the office. Since he needed to have his accountant go over them that evening, he turned around and headed back to the office.

About three-quarters of an hour after Fred left, Hank decided to finish his paperwork at home. He unplugged the adding machine, tucked it under his arm, and started to leave. At that moment, Fred came back, saw the adding machine under Hank's arm, and accused him of trying to steal it. Hank bristled, and the two men got into a heated argument. Fred ended the argument by informing Hank that his services would no longer be wanted.

On his way home, Hank consoled himself, "At least that Fred will never deprive me of my income again."

He couldn't have been more wrong.

Family Relationships and Homelife

No More Truckin'

Hank was proud of his rig. He and his trucks, he felt, had always taken care of his wife.

The big truck driver was coasting down a hill. As he tapped his brakes, they did not respond. Realizing that he would continue to pick up speed, Hank made his decision. He brought his rig to a halt by plowing into the side of a hill. The impact flipped the truck as though it were a coin.

The doctor gave Hank the news. He would be permanently disabled. The patient wondered what he would say to the wife who depended on him.

Upon receiving the doctor's report, Dorothy read her husband's thoughts. "Don't worry, honey. You've taken good care of me all these years. Now it's my turn to take care of you."

The couple remembered the wedding vows they had spoken—for better or worse, in sickness and in health.

The beautiful part is that, after all the years, they still remembered them.

Polly Wants Cracker

Polly stared unhappily out the window. She was deeply troubled about her relationship with her husband "Cracker." His unbelief in God was getting Polly down. She felt sure that her twelve-year-old marriage was on the rocks. She did not look forward to seeing her beloved little family broken up.

Polly suddenly burst into tears and prayed, "Dear God, please save our little family." To herself, she wondered if her prayer was heard. She needn't have wondered; God hears all heartfelt prayers.

Last week, I was privileged to witness the most inspiring church service I have yet attended. After the pastor dedicated Polly and Cracker's children to the Lord, I then saw an even greater miracle. Polly and Cracker were simultaneously baptized.

Peter's still-relevant statement came to my mind:

> Wives, fit in with your husband's plans;
>
> for ten if they refuse to listen when you
>
> talk to them about the Lord, they will be
>
> won by your respectful, pure behavior.
>
> You Godly lives will speak to them better
>
> than any words. (1 Pet. 3:1–2)

Wha-Wha-What's Wrong with Him?

Ricky was rather small for his age and was many times excluded from the bigger boys' games. Whenever he was rebuffed, he would turn to his mother.

"Mom-mom-mommy, why won't they let me p-p-play with them?"

"If you'd stop your stupid stuttering, maybe you'd make some friends." The woman's outbursts would upset the little lad even more. He was becoming gradually more withdrawn and shier.

One afternoon, over coffee, Delores remarked to her closest friend, "Ricky hardly ever talks to me anymore. It sure is hard to love someone who doesn't talk to you. I wonder what's wrong with him?"

The Measure You Give

When Jeff was five years old, he displeased his mother. When his father heard of the displeasure, he removed his belt as a prelude to the usual bare-skinned punishment for the boy.

Jeff, still sore from an earlier encounter, cried and pleaded with his father not to hit him that time. He father issued an ultimatum: accept the usual punishment or be object of silence forever.

Jeff, unable to bear any more physical abuse, elected for the latter choice. This was a difficult decision because he was an only child and his mother forbade him to ever have a friend over or to visit a friend.

A few days later, after dinner, Jeff wanted to show his father the latest additions to his stamp collection. The collection consisted of two small envelopes of postage stamps. One look at his father's face reminded him of the agreement for silence.

A few days afterward, Jeff's father was painting the springs of a mattress. Jeff thought it would be fun to help and asked if he could. His father's silence reminded Jeff of his nonexistence.

Jeff could bear it no longer; he went into the bedroom, got a belt, and asked his dad to use it on him. Jeff had learned his lesson . . . maybe too well.

Eleven years later, Frank and Eunice (Jeff's parents) were divorced. Jeff remained with his father, for his mother left the state. The blame for the divorce fell on Jeff's shoulders—literally and figuratively. In a way, Jeff was glad for the divorce. He could now visit his friends at their house or have them over to his whenever he wished.

About six months after the divorce, Frank was taking Jeff and Les, Jeff's friend, to the beach. It was very hot, and the boys were anxious to get there. Jeff noticed that his father was driving much slower than the posted speed limit. Jeff asked him to speed up a little.

In response to Jeff's request, his father slowed down even more. Everyone on the freeway was looking at them, and Jeff was afraid his father would get a ticket for breaking the minimum speed law.

Halfway to the beach, Jeff's father pulled off the freeway to stop at a junkyard. It seemed he needed a hood emblem for his car. The boys waited in the car for over an hour. When they became thirsty, Jeff went to buy a bottle of soda pop for them to share. (Les had no money.)

Upon returning to the car, Jeff heard a commotion. His father, in a rage, told him that while he was gone, his friend Les had given him a piece of his mind. He then accused Jeff of putting Les up to it. Frank turned the car around and headed for home.

On the way, Frank told Jeff that he and Les could never see each other again. Jeff was instructed to come straight home from school every day until further notice. He was not to leave the house for any reason, and the telephone service was disconnected so that no calls could be made or received.

In addition to this, Jeff was to turn over any money he might receive in the mail from his relatives to Frank. If he disobeyed any of these terms, Frank would put him in a home for wayward boys and would refuse to let him graduate from high school.

Jeff was an honor student. Jeff accepted the terms in silence; he had no choice. Besides, the following week was Easter vacation, and he was sure his dad would lighten up.

Come Easter vacation, his dad would not relent and further ordered Jeff to attend church with him every day of that week. On the way home from church one morning, Frank asked Jeff if he would like to have breakfast at a nearby restaurant.

Jeff reminded his father that he was without funds. His father offered to loan Jeff some money. Jeff refused and reminded Frank that he was holding fifteen dollars of his son's money.

When they arrived home, Jeff went to his room to stare at the walls. Twenty minutes later, the door opened. Frank placed the fifteen dollars on the desk and rescinded all the other terms of punishment. Frank asked Jeff to go grocery shopping with him and Jeff said yes. On the way to the store, Frank asked Jeff if he would like to stop at Les's house and pick him up too. Jeff happily agreed.

The Room

With the help of a friend, Larry set up an experiment in mental machinations. Larry had his friend lock him in a room for a day. This was no ordinary room; it had no windows, and the door was locked from the outside. There were no appliances in the room, nor was there a telephone. The walls were devoid of pictures or color; the floor was a slab of cement. There was no reading material in the room, nor any light to read by.

Larry sat down against a wall, with a smile of contentment on his face. "At least," he said aloud, "total privacy. No distractions, no bad news or contact with the world." (The room had a soundproof ceiling.) Several hours went by, and Larry was in a state of tranquility.

After about four hours (no watch or clock to be certain), Larry began to think that a picture on one wall would, at least, relieve the monotony of the room. After another hour or two, Larry wished he had something to read. When he realized there was nothing to read, he wished there were just one window so he could at least see what was going on outside. After about eight hours, Larry wished he could telephone his wife to make sure she was all right.

A short time later, Larry saw the doorknob move. He jumped up, smiled at his friend, and was glad to be out of the room.

The Birth

During Elizabeth's pregnancy, Eddie wondered why he did not have the wonderful feeling of anticipation that all his friends, relatives, and in-laws had over the coming birth. They all kidded him about his lack of enthusiasm over the coming event. Since manufacturing feelings that weren't really there seemed hypocritical to him, he kept pretty silent about the entire matter.

Finally, the day came. Unlike all the fathers-to-be we have seen in the movies and on television, Eddie stayed outwardly calm. Although he was starting to feel a few butterflies, he then put Elizabeth's suitcase (which had been packed and ready to go for two weeks) into their car.

He called the obstetrician, who said he would meet them at the hospital in half an hour. Lastly, he called Elizabeth's mother and took Elizabeth to the hospital. On the way there, unlike our celluloid heroes, he obeyed all traffic laws and signals.

After filling out various forms, he went to the cafeteria for coffee. There would be no pacing or cigarette puffing for Eddie. Before his second cup of coffee was gone, a nurse came in and told him to come and see his newborn daughter.

After seeing her and spending a few quiet moments with his wife, he got into his car and headed toward home. He made two stops on the way—flowers for his wife and the smallest pink dress he could find for his daughter to wear home from the hospital.

Upon arriving home, he was filled with a warm feeling of love and responsibility for his newly born daughter. He thanked God for the living gift with which he had been presented; he was thankful for her health and her mother's health. He sensed that his life would somehow never be the same.

Eddie has enjoyed the ensuing ten years of joys and also responsibilities of fatherhood. He found out that he was right about something—his life hasn't been the same, and he wouldn't want it any other way.

Sojourn in Solo

As Mike's senses took in the panoramic beauty of Oregon's Crater Lake, he knew that seeing it with his wife and daughter greatly enhanced the experience. As he focused on the blue-green beauty of its peaceful water, his mind wandered back to another sight that the forces of nature had once displayed for him.

It was spring 1967. Mike was driving from California to South Dakota to visit some old friends. As he proceeded north through Wyoming, he realized that he had not seen another vehicle on the highway for many miles.

When he reached the top of a steep grade, he could see the majestic mosaic before him. There was snow all around, as far as could be seen. The road ahead stretched toward a snow-covered mountain peak, which disappeared in a seeming eternity of pure and puffy white clouds. Mike wished he had someone with whom to share his joy.

Seven years later, surrounded by the beauty of nature and his own family, he silently thanked God for granting his wish.

Jesus Was a Teenager

A consensus seems to indicate that parent-child relationships undergo the most severe tests during the progeny's teen years.

Teenagers prefer adult treatment but, on occasion, still act like children. To complicate matters, the feelings behind the actions are genuine. What can one do when involved in this situation? While no specific action is all-encompassing, a little understanding can go a long way.

The teenager should keep in mind that parents deserve something in return for the love and support they have given. Parents would do well to try some mental exercise. An unfolding of the memory will remind them that, at a similar age, their behavior was probably less than perfect.

Men and women become parents of teenagers because they survived their own adolescence. If all these insights do not improve the relationship, we would all do well to consider this:

Jesus was a teenager.

Hairy Harry

Janet and Harry and been married for many years.

Harry was rather hairy. Lately, his wife had been complaining about the amount of hair that she was finding in the tub. Upon arriving home from work, Harry was greeted with these words: "I'm sick and tired of the way you've been leaving the bathtub. I wish I would never have to clean up after you again. Why don't you get out of here?"

The hapless husband obliged his irate mate.

Since Janet was unwilling to work, she had applied for family assistance. Now, the taxpayers of her state have been presented with the opportunity of keeping her bathtub clean. Aren't they lucky?

I'm a Nursery

For an exercise in self-awareness, Larry was asked which inanimate object he would be willing to spend his life as. Before the following day, he must think of a reply.

That night, Larry dreamt that he was a nursery. He saw his daughter being brought home for the first time. He heard the child say her first words and watched as she took her first steps.

The nursery was filled with the sound of laughter as the little girl and her friends grew up together; no music was sweeter. Physical, mental, and spiritual development were ongoing processes which the nursery was privileged to sense.

Upon awaking, Larry knew what his answer would be.

Slumber Party

Little girls spending the night
is, oh, such a beautiful sight!
Adding to our family of three,
watching nature films on the TV.

Pure hearts and innocent faces—
time doesn't pass; it just races.
Eating popcorn down on the floor,
only yesterday, they were four.

Telling little stories and tales
keeps plenty of wind in their sails.
Giggling instead of sleeping,
happy hearts planting and reaping

Then yours spends the night; in return,
some things from their peers, they must learn.
Next, she's back under her cherished dome;
what a blessing to have her back home.

Why Jacks Are Wild

Coffee mug in hand, the man surveyed the interior of his garage. For a long time, he'd been wanting to put up storage shelves. Knowing about this father's plans, Jack "borrowed" several sheets of plywood from a nearby construction site.

The mischievous teenager screeched into the driveway, "Hey, Dad. I got you some free plywood."

As the man finished his last sip of coffee, his wife came into the garage to take some clothes out of the dryer. Seeing the two men unloading the plywood, she inquired as to where they had gotten it. Upon hearing the facts, Jack's mother recommended that the boy's father punish him; she did not approve of stealing in any form.

For his punishment, Jack was to spend the remainder of the evening in his room. While confined to his room, the sixteen-year-old enjoyed his television and stereo; they were "stern" reminders of his punishment.

As he was getting ready for bed, Jack's father stuck his head inside his son's bedroom. "By the way, Jack, thanks a lot for the plywood."

A Little Boy

There was a little boy

who liked his boat.

He loved to swim,

and he loved to float.

But whether on land

or sailing his yacht,

he was thankful to God

for everything he got.

As he swung in the part

and listened to a lark,

he would smile and grin

while he played with his friend.

With his siblings, he'd share

everything that he had;

he is loved and enjoyed

by this mom and his dad.

Shamed by Sugar

Have you ever felt that something's missing when you're not surrounded by gadgets and diversions? I have.

Today, I watched our family pet. She is a kitten named Sugar. I watched her enjoy the warmth of the morning sun. I watched her enjoy the coolness of the evening's shade. She was happy just to walk on the earth. Her playmates were the trees, the leaves, and the wind. She devoured her food with a relish and found plain old water the most satisfying. She has learned not to waste nor take for granted.

Even Jesus, when He miraculously supplied over five thousand people with bread, allowed none to be wasted. We have learned much from studying about Jesus; we can learn a little by observing Sugar.

Break Time

"Oh, why do I have to be stuck at home with this miserable cold?" Rita moaned. "Not only can't I go to work, but I'm even too sick to accomplish anything here at home."

Since Rita enjoyed her active lifestyle, staying at home was especially hard on her. During the next several days, the woman resigned herself to her bed rest. For the first time in years, she was able to read a book without interruption.

In an effort to vary her surroundings, she spent several hours a day in a different room. She observed each room as if for the first time. She decided that the time and money spent on decorations was now returning dividends on cheer to her. She was able to reexperience the joy of looking unhurriedly at her son's papers when he came home from school.

Rita was almost beginning to enjoy her confinement. When she did return to work, it was with renewed vigor and a better perspective.

What I Should Have Said

Recently, I had to drive my wife to a distant city to pick up some merchandise. Upon arriving, we found that we had been given an incorrect address.

After driving around the city for a short time, I blurted, "Why did you have to bother me with this anyway?"

Seeing the hurt expression on her face, I promptly offered an apology. Although she quickly and graciously accepted, words can never really be erased.

That evening, I tried to analyze my behavior. Why had I spoken the way I did to the person I love above all others? I was on a tight schedule, and the difficulty of acquiring gasoline had been increasing. Surely, there must have been a better way to handle the situation. I asked myself the age-old question—"What should I have said?"

Upon reflecting, I decided that I should have simply stated that circumstances were causing me to feel anxiety.

While it is not easy to verbalize such feelings, it would have been an improvement from the aforementioned accusatory manner.

Forgiveness

The Thief with a Soft Heart

Amos was a retired mechanic. Though he was retired, he used his time productively.

As the former mechanic drove along in his station wagon, his eyes alertly scanned the curbs. Amos was looking for discarded bicycles. It was his custom to haul them home and repair them.

After the repairs were completed, the kindly gentleman would bestow his gift upon someone in his community. He would usually choose a financially underprivileged child. Although a child's smile was sufficient reward for Amos, he would sometimes receive thank-you letters from his beneficiary. Our sentimental friend had a stack of these letters in his drawer.

The still-deft mechanic arrived home with a badly broken bicycle. As he was getting out of his wagon, a police car pulled unto his driveway.

"Does this vehicle belong to you, sir?" The officers asked.

"Yes, why do you ask?"

"Its license plate matches the number we were given by headquarters. Someone reported that its driver removed a bicycle from their premises."

"I did take a bicycle from someone's house just now. It was next to their trash cans, and I thought it was going to be thrown away."

"I'm sorry, sir, you'll have to come with us."

At headquarters, Amos tried to explain how many times he had done this same thing. The sergeant told him that he would have to remain in custody unless he could somehow prove that his intentions were not those of a criminal.

Amos phoned his wife. "Hello, Peg, do you know about the stack of thank-you letters that I keep in my drawer?"

"You mean the ones I keep on telling you to throw away?"

"Yes, please ring them to the police station right away. I need them."

After examining several dozen letters from grateful youngsters, the sergeant told Amos he was free to leave.

As Peggy and Amos were about to leave, the sergeant called out, "Wait a minute! I've got an old, beat-up bicycle at home. Would you like me to bring it over to hour house after I get off duty?"

The good-natured thief winked. "You bet I would."

Forgive and Forget?

We have all heard the expression "Forgive and forget."

While, as Christians, we must forgive; it is usually more difficult to forget. When we find that we are unable to forget, we sometimes feel a sense of guilt. Guilt will not help us forget; it will only make matters worse. I believe that the recollection of negative experiences can sometimes be used in positive ways.

In the book of Acts, Gamaliel was able to defend the apostles and save their lives by recounting to the Pharisees how the followers of Theudas and the followers of Judas the Galilean had been scattered. Apparently, the Pharisees had felt threatened by those men too. If Gamaliel had not recalled these previous uprisings, the apostles would have been put to death. Since the apostles were partly responsible for the conversion of many, should Gamaliel not receive some of the credit for helping to keep them alive?

In Matthew 23:37–39, Jesus says,

> "Jerusalem, Jerusalem! You kill the
> prophets and stone the messengers God
> has sent you! How many times I wanted
> to put my arms around all your people,

just as a hen gathers her chicks under her wings, but you would not let me! And so your temple will be abandoned and empty. From now on, I tell you, you will never see me again until you say 'God bless him who comes in the name of the Lord.'"

While Jesus expressed a desire to forgive, the very words He uttered prove that He had not forgotten the wrongs of a rebellious people.

Healed

Mario didn't really dislike Sophia, but he didn't really like her either. Among other things, Sophia was always turning on the air conditioner or plugging in the fan. To Mario, this made the office too cold for comfort.

Now, Mario was feeling sick. He didn't say anything, but he was pretty sure that Sophia was responsible.

Oh well, what's the difference? he thought to himself. *Next week, she's going to retire.*

Sophia, noticing that Mario didn't look very well, offered him some medicine. The usually stubborn son of an immigrant gratefully accepted her gracious offer. In a couple of hours, he began to feel a little better.

At the office retirement party, the two people embraced warmly. Mario had been healed in more ways than one.

Settle with Your Opponent

Upon returning to work after the New Year weekend, I was approached by one of my fellow workers during our coffee break. He sat down and told me that he went to a New Year's Eve party.

While the party was in progress, he got into a fight with one of the other partygoers. He sent the man to the hospital with a broken jaw. The man was now suing him for medical expenses and lost time from work.

Upon hearing the story, I immediately remembered the words contained in Luke 12:58–59:

> If someone brings a lawsuit against you
> and takes you to court, do your best to
> settle the dispute with him before you get
> to court. If you don't, he will drag you
> before the judge, who will hand you over
> to the police, and you will be put in jail.
> There you will stay, I tell you, until you
> pay the last penny of your fine.

Sensing that he wanted my advice, I relayed this golden nugget from the Book of books to him. He must have thought it was a good idea, for he said he would try to follow the advice.

At this writing, the outcome of this matter is still uncertain. One thing, however, is certain: the words of Jesus are still as applicable in 1979 as they were when He first taught them in His usual spirit of love. He did not give us His Father's teaching to keep us from having fun; He gave them to us for our own protection.

The Church Is Burning!

Disgusted over his financial plight, the man pored over the newspaper. Several of the articles he had read recently gave him the impression that churches were all getting rich at the people's expense.

Very early Sunday morning, the man did something that had not done in years—he went to church. Upon seeing the church empty, the man lit a match, tossed it down, and walked out. Miraculously, the damage was not as severe as it might have been.

Four weeks later, the unemployed man decided to vent his frustrations again. This time, he lit two matches and placed them more strategically. Again, miraculously, the church was not completely destroyed. By the following morning, the embittered man had decided that divine providence must be on the side of the church.

A few days later, desperation drove him to the church. He asked the pastor if a custodial position were open. The pastor hired him.

After three months, the man could no longer bear his guilt. He burst into the pastor's office and announced, "I quit! I can't take it anymore."

"But why?" the pastor asked. "You're doing such a good job here."

"You don't understand," the man pleaded. "I'm the one who tried to burn down your church!"

The pastor looked into the tortured man's eyes. "I know" was all he said.

Future

Double-Check Discards

It is a truism that we should think twice before we discard something of possible value. In the fifties, I collected baseball cards. I had the complete 1954 and 1957 sets. I threw them away in the sixties. A friend of mine, who still collects baseball cards, told me that my collection could have been sold at the last trade convention for three or four thousand dollars.

I also collected phonograph records in the fifties and sixties. I gave away hundreds of records in the midsixties in an effort to make room for the newer, more important music.

Recently, I remembered how much I enjoyed those old songs and tried to buy replacement copies. I had to pay much more per copy than I did originally, and most of the records were no longer available, at any price.

The point is this: before you toss away possessions, words, friends, careers, religious values, or marriages, stop to consider their value (current or potential).

Environmental Exercise

While driving home from work some months ago, I looked upon a construction site, with accustomed chagrin. Being an environmentalist, I feel pangs of pain whenever I see a field being filled in. My face showed frowns and furrows as the building progressed.

Recently, my daughter decided she would like to take gymnastic lessons. I looked in the telephone book and copied down the address of the only gymnastics club listed.

As I drove toward our destination, the area looked very familiar. Upon arriving, I realized that the building that would bring so much joy to my daughter rested upon my once-cherished field.

In the future, I hope we will consider the potential value of something before downgrading it.

The Gift of Tomorrow

If you have quarreled,

tomorrow may bring reconciliation.

If you are sick,

tomorrow may bring a return to health.

If you are lonely,

tomorrow may bring a new friend.

If you have fallen behind in your work,

tomorrow you may catch up.

If you have too much time on your hands,

tomorrow you can donate some.

If you are low on money,

tomorrow may bring a windfall.

If your land is too dry,

tomorrow may bring rain.

If you have had too much rain,

tomorrow may be sunny and bright.

If your heart or an appliance is broken,

tomorrow it may be repaired.

If you have been thwarted by some obstacle,

tomorrow it may be removed.

If you are upset,

tomorrow you may receive a visit from the

Prince of peace.

Don't Sweat the Small Stuff

Since Vern became a saved Christian, he had no fear of death. He did not possess any of the other major fears as well. What really bothered Vern was the little things in life—e.g., the search for gasoline. This otherwise pillar of strength asked me if I had any advice to offer him on minute matters.

Having no words of my own to offer him, I borrowed the words of Jesus:

> So don't worry about having enough food
> and clothing. Why be like the heathen?
> For they take pride in all these things and
> are deeply concerned about them. But your
> heavenly Father already knows perfectly
> well that you need them, and He will give
> them to you if you give Him first place in
> your life as He wants you to. So don't be
> anxious about tomorrow. God will take
> care of tomorrow too. Live one day at a
> time. (Matt. 6:31–34)

The Living End

During the 1950s, a religious leader informed me that the world would end in 1960. Not wanting to miss out on any fun, I spent the remainder of the decide living it up.

More recently, another "religious leader" intimated the earth would cease rotating on May 1, 1979. Foolish me! I continued to pay my bills and mow the lawn. But perhaps I was not so foolish; it is now October (at this writing).

Well then, if the end failed to arrive in 1960 and again on May 1, 1979, just when can we expect the occurrence? The answer can be found in the Bible. To save some the trouble of looking it up, this is what the Word says:

> No one knows, however, when that day
> or hour will come . . . neither the angels
> in heaven, nor the Son; only the Father
> knows. Be on watch, be alert, for you do
> not know when the time will come. (Mark
> 13:32–33)

The person who spoke those words was none other than Jesus Christ. We would save a lot of wear and tear on ourselves if we would listen to Him.

Gossip and Rumors

Miss Priss

Due to her aloofness and manner of walking, Stephanie was known among her coworkers as "Miss Priss."

It was only after many months that the truth became known . . . Stephanie had arteriosclerosis. Her deteriorating condition caused her to walk the only way she could walk.

As for her aloofness, she probably didn't want to burden anyone with her troubles.

Gossip leaves us with three options: offense, defense, or silence. Two of the three are usually more preferable—the latter two!

Who's Laughing Now?

In the early sixties, Henry's neighbors used to laugh at him. Henry was one of the early environmentalists. He rode a bicycle for short trips, and he always cut his lawn with a hand mower.

Sometimes, he would overhear his neighbor's derogatory comments, "What's the matter with Henry? Is he too cheap to buy a power mower? And what about that bicycle he rides? I'll bet his daughter has to stand in line, just to ride it."

Through it all, Henry tried to be patient; he knew that such comments resulted from ignorance. Besides, now that the general public has become aware of air pollution and energy shortages, he doesn't hear them laughing anymore.

Malignant Marriage

Dave and Nancy have managed to raise their children in a Christian manner and have seen those children graduate from college. Their children are happily married and have made Dave and Nancy proud grandparents. Dave and Nancy's children are engaged in their chosen careers and are quite happy. Doesn't it all sound wonderful?

This perfect picture is a domestic dream that has been clouded by reeking vapor of a rumor.

Nancy heard, through the grapevine, that Dave was being unfaithful to her. She believed this was true because Dave sometimes did get home an hour or two later than usual. But Nancy was too sophisticated to let Dave in on her suspicions. Instead, she decided to have an affair of her own.

After several months of extramarital involvement, guilt began to creep in. One day, when Nancy had experienced a very trying day, she told Dave the news about her revengeful adventures.

Upon hearing the news, Dave was shocked and hurt. Dave explained to Nancy that he had been working voluntary overtime to buy her a present for their upcoming wedding anniversary.

Nancy stubbornly clung to her suspicions and asked Dave for a divorce. Dave agreed to a trial separation until he could sort out his thoughts and feeling.

After living alone for several months, Dave is considering having an affair of his own—just to even the score a little before deciding on his plans for the future.

What effect will the repercussions have on Dave and Nancy's grandchildren? On themselves? On other people involved?

In retrospect, poor means of communications seems to be the culprit in this marital decline.

But what about the future? Where are the answers to be found regarding that?

I believe the answers to these and other problems confronting people can be found in deep prayer and in reading the Bible.

Greed

False Profit

Oliver was proud to be the new owner/manager of a small mobile home park. He congratulated himself on his business transaction and vowed to reap large dividends on his investment.

Through research, Oliver found that more rent could be charged if there were no children on the premises. A search of his rental contracts revealed only one family with children. Oliver initiated a campaign to oust them so he could begin making some real dough' A lengthy legal entanglement resulted.

Upon arriving home, Oliver asked his wife, "Have you heard any news from the attorney today?"

"No," she countered. "But I did hear some news from the doctor. I'm pregnant!"

The Odds Are with Me

Jim reclined in his bus seat, gazing out at the countryside. He was looking forward to spending the night in a Nevada fun spot.

Upon arriving at his destination, he checked into his reserved room. After a shower and change of clothes, Jim enjoyed a very entertaining dinner show. When the show was over, he headed for the two-dollar black jack table. Jim still had a hundred dollars and only needed twenty-five for his return ticket.

As soon as he sat down, he felt it would be his lucky night. After two hours, he had doubled his money. Then he decided to try his luck at the five-dollar tables. He did even better there.

After a couple of more hours, he had quadrupled his original stake. Jim decided to try the twenty-five dollar table just for fun. Jim hit a dry stretch and within half an hour was back down to his original hundred dollars.

After two more straight losses, he was down to his last two chips. He placed his bet and smiled as the dealer gave him a nineteen. When the dealer showed twenty, Jin's smile disappeared. He was down to his transportation money. Jim got up and started to walk away.

Then he heard a voice whisper, *"Don't quit while you're a loser. The dealer was lucky to beat your last hand. And after four consecutive losses, the odds are with you."*

"Yes," Jim answered himself, "the odds are with me."

He returned to the table and plunked down his last chip. He was dealt a king and a jack; with twenty points in his hand, Jim was sure he couldn't lose. When the dealer turned over twenty-one, Jim stared in disbelief.

Walking along, with his thumb out, Jim had traveled several miles without attracting a ride. He went into a gas station for a drink of water. Sitting on the curb, in front of the station, Jim began to worry. "What if I don't get home in time for work Monday? I may lose my job." He thought of calling in sick to cover himself, but he didn't have enough change for the telephone.

Suddenly, he jumped up—a ride at last!

As Jim got into the car, he said, "Thanks a lot for the ride, buddy. I didn't make out so good at the tables. Oh well, maybe I'll have better luck next time."

Managerial Mayhem

Fran, the new waitress, seemed to be all thumbs. To make matters worse, the restaurant's manager continually barked orders to her. No matter how hard she tried, she could not seem to please Mr. Simmons.

As Fran hurriedly cleared the table, she reached for the jar of mustard. Grabbing the jar by its lid, she was startled to see it go crashing to the floor. Apparently, the table's last occupants had not replaced the lid securely.

As Fran bent over to clean up the slippery mess, Mr. Simmons came running over. "Don't bother with that now. There's a dozen people waiting for a table. Hurry up and seat them so we can start making money off them."

"But, Mr. Simmons," Fran pleaded, "somebody's liable to slip and hurt themselves. They might even sue!"

"Let me worry about that," the manager intoned. "You go wait on the customers."

As the young couple headed toward the table, the husband noticed the potential hazard; but before he could warn his wife, she slipped quickly on the floor.

Mr. Simmons came running over. "Please excuse the mess, I assure you, the person responsible will pay for his negligence!"

The husband, who had witnessed the entire proceedings, looked the manager in the eye. "You bet your bottom dollar *you* will!"

Guilt

The Guilty Widow

Helen was complaining to some of the women in her office.

"My husband, Harvey, is under doctor's orders to stay inside and avoid physical exertion. He was forced into early retirement, due to heart and respiratory problems. Now, we can never go out together. I wish I could have some fun, like other wives do."

That evening, as Helen turned the corner, she saw an ambulance in front of her house. One look at the sheet-covered figure of her former husband told the story.

Helen became almost hysterical and ran to her neighbor's house. As she paced the floor, nervously puffing a cigarette, she repeated over and over, "Oh, why did I have to complain about Harvey at work this morning? Now I feel so guilty!"

Since Helen does not believe in Jesus, she has no one to free her from her guilt. Isn't it a shame?

Hatred
and
Hostility

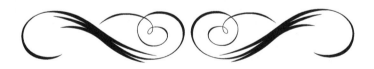

Facing the Music

Stewart loved to play his stereo at full blast. He knew that it disturbed his neighbors, but that only seemed to add to his enjoyment.

One day, the music lover forgot to lock his door upon leaving. While he was gone for the day, someone entered his apartment and transformed his thirty albums into sixty pieces.

Stewart is now the unhappy owner of the quietest stereo in town.

Prey Always

No, I did not make a typographical error! This is a story about predators and their prey.

Scott was proud of his newly acquired acreage. As he surveyed his property, he noticed a coyote near his border. Feeling very protective of his livestock, Scott decided to shoot every rattlesnake and hawk in the area.

Scott was proud of his efforts to exterminate all predators; he despised them intensely. Though he was not a vegetarian, Scott did not view himself as a predator.

With most of the predators gone, Scott began to experience a genuine problem. The rodent population began to soar; his grain and crops were being ravaged. To find and kill them all would be an impossible mission.

In a state of bewilderment, the murderous man turned on his television. After accidentally viewing a wildlife film, Scott shook his head ruefully. "I think I know how to get rid of those rodents . . . too bad I killed all my predatory friends."

Strategy

In his account of the Gospel, Luke tells us that Pilate and Herod were enemies. After Pilate handed Jesus over to Herod, the two men became friends. Does this story have any relevance in today's world?

Carol and Bruce didn't particularly care for each other, but they decided to unite for a common cause. They knew that Kevin and a physical problem. They decided to conspire, in an effort to knock Kevin out of his desk job and out into the workroom.

Having succeeded, they smirked as they saw Kevin's face mirrored in pain. Kevin had tried to "hang in there," but he was physically unable to meet the demands of the workroom. Kevin had to file for an early medical retirement.

Now that Kevin was gone, Carol and Bruce were able to do what they liked best—make life miserable for each other.

Blown Away

Buddy was a mischievous boy. He liked to blow great, big bubbles with his gum and then let the bubble burst repeatedly with loud pops. He did this because he knew that others around him were bothered by the sound. Buddy got a big kick out of bothering people. To use his own words, "It really blows me away to upset everyone."

One night, Buddy had a dream. He dreamed that he had blown the biggest bubble of his life. But instead of bursting, it grew to mammoth proportions. He felt himself being lifted off the ground.

As he ascended toward the stratosphere, he looked down and saw all his friends smiling and waving goodbye to him.

Real Gone Graffiti

It was lunchtime, and Rudy headed for the men's lounge to comb his hair. Rudy was very displeased at the way his supervisor, Mr. Jackson, had been treating him. Rudy, a coward, would not speak directly to Mr. Jackson about his alleged mistreatment; instead, he chose to attack the boss with his knife.

Oh, he wouldn't stab him with it; he would just carve something nasty about him into the wall. Rudy didn't use a pen or pencil because he wanted to leave a more permanent memorial to Mr. Jackson. Among his close friends, Rudy referred to his boss as Lurch (after The Addams Family character).

A couple of hours later, Luke, the custodian, came in to service the men's lounge. He washed all the graffiti off the walls—all except Rudy's (since he wasn't carrying an electric sanding machine).

Late that afternoon, Rudy whispered to his friends a little too loudly, "Cool it! Here comes Lurch."

"Lurch" overheard Rudy and said to him, "So you're the one who carved 'Lurch is a jerk' into the wall. Get your things, Rudy. You're fired."

Rudy had cut himself with his own knife.

Leroy the Loser

Buddy had moved around a lot, and entering a new school always made him feel somewhat insecure. The year was 1958, and Buddy had just entered a new high school in Los Angeles, California. Buddy was anxious to be accepted by his peers, but because of his New York background, he was slow to be accepted.

Buddy noticed Leroy on the first day of his freshman year. Leroy did not appear to be very popular with his classmates, and Buddy was quick to take advantage of the situation. Buddy took an instant dislike to Leroy. He called Leroy a loser and other insulting names. He never passed up an opportunity to ridicule Leroy or to pick a fight with him. Although Leroy had not done anything wrong to anyone, Buddy constantly tried to turn Leroy's classmates against him; he also encouraged them to pick fights with Leroy.

One Friday afternoon, there was an after-school basketball game. Buddy wanted to stay and watch it, but it was a rule that he call his mother if he intended to be late. Buddy had no money and started asking his friends for a dime to place a telephone call.

When none of his friends had the necessary coin, Leroy volunteered to give Buddy the ten cents. Buddy really wanted to see this particular basketball game, so he accepted Leroy's kind offer.

Thereafter, Buddy thought to himself, *The real loser hasn't been Leroy—the real loser has been me.*

Common Scents

Dick had been at his job for a long time; he hated it, and everyone connected with it. The disgruntled employee never confronted anyone with his hostile feelings; he was not on speaking terms with everyone. Over the years, Dick had purposely neglected his personal hygiene in order to keep people away from himself.

Although everyone was too nice to offend him by saying anything about this lack of consideration, they all wondered how he was able to tolerate himself!

Idleness

What! Me Work?

Gary was the manager of the Donna Beth Apartments in Azusa, California. To make ends meet, Gary also held another full-time position. The hours were midnight until eight thirty in the morning.

As Gary was leaving for work, at ten minutes 'til midnight, he noticed many of the tenants drinking and smoking and were sitting around the swimming pool. The manager wondered how they could afford luxuries, since many of them had not been paying their rent.

The next day, the manager set about his rent-collecting duties. The poolside patrons all gave him the same answer: "I don't have any money. I'm unemployed."

Gary asked them if they would like him to get them a job at his place of employment.

Their response was unanimous: "What! And work lousy hours like you?"

Rape!

Rocky and his friends belonged to a street gang. Rocky was proud to be the Red Wings' leader. Besides gang wars, vandalism, booze, drugs, and petty theft, the gang had an initiation rite.

Before a new member was accepted, he had to rape someone. The usual procedure was for the gang to meet in the city's largest park. After they were all gathered together, Rocky would inform the prospective member to attack the first female to come along.

On this particular night, everything was set up as usual. The young men hid behind a large tree, and Rocky gave the command; the order was instantly obeyed.

When it was all over, Rocky was stunned to see that the girl was his younger sister.

Inspiration
and
Encouragement

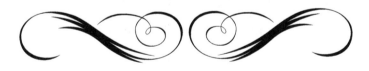

True Happiness

Maintaining a trouble-free mind

by never being unkind.

Helping a friend in need,

instead of watching him bleed.

Drying a tear with tissue,

instead of pressing the issue.

Obstacles finally overcome,

so a happy tune, you hum.

Quiet moments with our spouse,

feel love radiating the house.

Watching your children grow,

now a deer, but first a doe.

Feeling His presence at all times,

even when you're out of rhymes.

Even through you've misbehaved,

it's bliss to know you're saved.

Charge

Pulling the car into the garage without letting the cat outside proved to be a hectic feat. In my haste, I forgot to turn off my headlights. The next morning, I was victimized by the inevitable dead battery; my important mission would have to be delayed.

In a quandary, I asked a friend to let me charge my battery by attaching a jumper cable to hers. Because of her graciousness, I was able to accomplish my mission.

Many times, our spiritual batteries run low. It is then that I am thankful for sources of renewal. Churches, prayer, and inspirational literature are some of the ways I recharge my spiritual batteries.

Which methods do you utilize?

Prison of Pain

Has the length and degree of your pain

made your whole life seem in vain?

'Tis a shame, since our stay is so brief;

we must suffer and carry our grief.

But what's worse—it's become automatic

to be labeled a "psychosomatic."

I wonder if things were reversed;

would the diagnosis be so perverse?

And when it's so bad you can't sleep,

someone tell you to smile, not to weep.

Like Job, you can't chuckle or grin

while accused of committing a sin.

We won't always feel so low;

there will come an end to our woe.

Thank God we will get some relief—

when we're sitting up there with the Chief!

Fingernails

Have you ever felt that you were hanging on by your fingernails? Well then, thank God for your fingernails!

Several months ago at work, I was called into the office. I was told that, due to my physical handicap, I could no longer work there. Even though I could perform better than most, I would no longer be allowed to support my family!

Well, this situation has still not been resolved, but through a series of prayers and miracles, I am still working there. Throughout the ongoing ordeal, some of my Christian friends comforted me with the idea that if I really had faith, I'd be healed. Was Lazarus healed by exercising his faith? It is difficult to exercise anything when you've been dead and buried for four days!

Surprisingly, much of my support and understanding came from agnostic acquaintances! Is it possible that without ever having read the Bible, they have received its message?

"So then, everything depend, not on what man wants or does, but only on God's mercy" (Rom. 9:16).

Fame and Fortune

There is a school of thought within certain Christian circles that to be a Christian is to be on the road to fame, fortune, and physical health. While I am sure that such a philosophy has brought many into the fold, I am equally sure that it has left some in a state of bewilderment. We are told that full commitment and right living produces every good thing. Should we be left with the "what's wrong with me" feeling?

In the remainder of this article, I will attempt to let the Bible explain why the answer is *no*.

Fame. During Jesus's earthly ministry, Jesus was known only within a radius of two hundred miles (hardly the qualifications for a celebrity). However, after his temporary demise, His following is now universal.

Fortune. Was Jesus wealthy? Jesus once had to send Peter fishing in order to reel in enough money to pay His tax. In 1 Timothy 6:5–10, Paul tells us,

> They think that religion is a way to become rich. Well, religion does make a person very rich, if he is satisfied with what he has. What did we bring into the world? Nothing! What can we take out of the

world? Nothing! So then, if we have food and clothes, that should be enough for us. But those who want to get rich fall into temptation and are caught in the trap of many foolish and harmful desires, which pull them down to ruin and destruction. For the love of money is a source of all kinds of evil. Some have been so eager to have it, that they have wandered away from the faith and have broken their hearts with many sorrows. (GNB)

The two great commandments call for love of God and people; the love of money is not mentioned. To further illustrate, Is everyone who is famous, rich, or physically sound a Christian? I know some who are not.

Physical health. When Jesus healed the ten lepers, only one came back to give thanks. If they were all so pious and spiritually aware, why did they not all come back?

Paul, one of God's most hardworking ambassadors, had a physical affliction. Shall we accuse him of a lack of faith because his wasn't healed? Certainly not.

While the nails were being driven in, Jesus was not in a very good state of physical health. Within hours, his health had deteriorated into death (temporary). Shall we say he did not have enough faith? Not I.

(Scriptural Reference: 2 Timothy 4:3)

The Sparrow and the Hawk

The sight always leaves me feeling amused—the mighty hawk being pestered and pecked at by a little sparrow. While the hawk is stronger and mightier than the sparrow, it is somewhat defenseless while soaring in the air. The hawk is vulnerable to attack from even small birds.

While Satan recognized that Jesus was stronger than he, this did not prevent him from attacking Jesus when He appeared vulnerable. After forty days and nights without food, Satan moved in with his message. Jesus defended Himself with scripture—God's message.

When we are vulnerable, we would do well to emulate Jesus. By filling our minds with the word of God, we will be able to resist many attacks.

Spiritual Seasons

In springtime,

we become reborn,

a time of transition—

caused by contrition.

In summer,

our spirit is filled with zeal,

our hearts are on fire—

the feeling is real.

In autumn,

when you would falter,

cling tight to the Lord—

your course, do not alter.

Then in the winter,

you'll run like a sprinter;

after you bid this world adieu—

you'll be given your life . . . to start it anew.

Guess Who Came to Dinner?

At age thirty-two, Larry decided to become baptized. Although he had been baptized as an infant, Larry decided it was time to make a conscious commitment to Christ. The ensuing two years found Larry absorbing as much as he could of the Bible; he also prayed and fasted.

One evening, after helping his wife clear the kitchen and dining room, he decided to retire early. When the alarm sounded at 3:00 a.m., Larry got dressed and started to leave for work. As he was putting on his jacket, he became aware of a soft glow emanating from the dining room.

Larry looked in that direction and saw the Lord sitting at the dining room table. There was a small round loaf of bread on a plate. The Lord appeared just as Larry had always pictured Him. He had long, brown hair and wore a beige-colored robe. No words were spoken; and when Larry looked again, the Lord, the bread, and the plate were gone.

A verse of scripture from the book of Revelation popped into Larry's mind: "Behold, I stand at the door and knock,. If anyone listens to My voice and opens the door, I shall come in to him and dine with him and he with Me" (Rev. 3:20).

Larry was so elated; he wanted to share the marvelous experience with everyone. However, he wondered if anyone would believe him. Did you?

Step Out

Many times, we would like to step out and proclaim the way of our Lord. Some of us are held back by the feeling that our knowledge or ability is too incomplete. I like to recall the story in Acts 18:24–28.

As it happened, a Jew named Apollos, a wonderful Bible teacher and preacher, had just arrived in Ephesus from Alexandria in Egypt. While he was in Egypt, someone had told him about John the Baptist and what John had said about Jesus, but that is all he knew. He had never heard the rest of the story!

So he was preaching boldly and enthusiastically in the synagogue, "The Messiah is coming! Get ready to receive Him!" Priscilla and Aquila were there and heard him, and it was a powerful sermon. Afterward, they met him and explained what had happened to Jesus since the time of John, and all that it meant!

Apollos had been thinking about going to Greece, and the believers encouraged him in this. They wrote to their fellow believers there, telling them to welcome him. And upon his arrival in Greece, he was greatly used of God to strengthen the church, for he powerfully refuted all the Jewish arguments in public debate, showing by the scriptures that Jesus is indeed the Messiah.

So, even when our knowledge is incomplete, God can use us!

Sunshine and Rain

While cutting our lawn yesterday, I noticed that the sections which received sunshine and rain had experienced the most growth. It is a truism—that in order for us to experience maximum growth, we must receive a combination of symbolic sunshine and rain.

President Abraham Lincoln, one of this country's greatest presidents, was defeated many times in his quest for public office.

While perusing my first hundred written stories and articles, I observed that about half were inspired by positive experiences; the other half were inspired by negative ones.

This is the time of year when we celebrate the resurrection of Jesus Christ. Let us all remember that before the resurrection came the crucifixion.

Maximize Your Strengths

All of us, since we are human, have one or more areas of weakness. Much specific advice is available on how to overcome almost any conceivable weakness. While much of this advice is helpful, let's examine the other end of the spectrum.

If we spend too much of our time dwelling on areas of weakness, we may be neglecting our strong points. To do this habitually is to do ourselves an injustice, and the method may even be counterproductive.

"A clay pot doesn't say to its maker, 'why did you make me this way?'" we learn in Romans 9:20–21.

The apostle Paul, with his usual insight, said it well: "Having done all, I stand" (Eph. 6:13).

Let's focus on more current events. A baseball player who hits more than an average number of home runs, but is a poor fielder, doesn't dwell on his weak point. He negotiates his contract on the basis of his strong point. If he continues to hit more than his share of home runs, he will not only be paid well, but he may wind up in baseball's hall of fame (every player's dream).

Likewise, if we utilize our strengths effectively, our weak points may seem miniscule or may even evaporate. Then we'll end up in the "ultimate hall of fame."

What's in Your Storage Room?

I believe much encouragement may be derived from the reading of Matthew 13:52. After the apostles expressed their understanding of some parables, Jesus likened them to authorize teachers and interpreters of the Old and New Testaments, although they had been following Him less than three years and were less than perfect in faith and wisdom. Some of us have been following the Lord longer than three years and have not become teachers.

Perhaps, some of us feel that we are not qualified because we lack ability or experience. I believe that familiarity with the Bible and a desire to help others may be the only necessary qualifications for a Sunday school teacher.

Although I was a relative newcomer to our church, I was asked if I would like to teach. Though I was willing to try, I felt less than qualified. Even after expressing these feelings of inadequacy, I found that I was still wanted.

After examining the curriculum, I rejected it as being too juvenile for young adults. Using only the Bible and my own experiences, I have been teaching junior and senior high Sunday school classes. Many times, I had no lesson prepared until Saturday night or Sunday morning. Somehow, even when working sixty hours a week, the Lord would give me just enough ideas to get us through one hour of Sunday school.

I have found the Sunday school hour to be the highlight of my week. It is a most enjoyable and rewarding experience, an experience for which I thank God. Perhaps, encouraged by this article, some of you will soon have a similar experience.

You are the Way You are
for a Reason

Sometimes, we agonize over situations or circumstances. Sometimes, we wonder why we are the way we are. A doctor who is also a trusted friend advised me thusly: "You are the way you are for a reason." I shall never forget the advice.

If we have done all we can to arrive at a state of change or a state of compromise, without result, why not try trusting God to use us just s we are?

If you feel your chosen career, physical state, financial state, lack of certain abilities, or heavy schedule is keeping you from being useful in Christian service, remember that God can put anyone to use.

In the Bible, the written record of God's dealing with all types of people were put to positive use. Thieves, murderers, and prostitutes—all became positive forces after they had asked for forgiveness. All that is really necessary is a desire to let God use us the way He sees fit.

Circular Motions

While doing some heavy cleaning the other day, I noticed that a circular motion accomplished more than a back and forth or up and down stroke. We in western culture have been led to believe in upward mobility—climbing the ladder of success. Many of us, when we feel we are not keeping pace with this conception, consider ourselves failures or misfits.

Eastern culture suffers no such hang-up for their philosophy is that life goes in cycles. If we could conceive of ourselves as being within a successful circle, thoughts of being on the low rungs of the ladder would be eliminated. With this attitude, chances for true success would be increased.

We must all remember that there are many forms of success. Many who have reached the pinnacle of fame and fortune have seen their family life and social relationships deteriorate beyond repair. I believe the meaning of true success can be found in John 16:33: "Cheer up, I have overcome the world."

Those words were uttered by Jesus; if we belong to Him, then we have already entered the cycle of eternal life. Is there anything on this earth that is more important?

Boats in the Harbor

The other night, I greeted my wife as she came home from night school. I expressed my concern about the demands being made on her. She takes excellent care of our daughter and me. She is a superior housekeeper; a good student; and spends much time helping her parents, friends, and neighbors. In addition to all that, she operates her own business. Quite a lot for a girl who, after being stricken with polio, was told she would never walk again.

After hearing me voice my concern, she then inspired the title for this story by saying, "Boats are safe in the harbor, but that's not the reason they were made." The statement was so typical of her—simple yet profound.

Many of us are content to leave our boats in the harbor rather than risk potential perils on the sea of life. I am told that most of us realize only 10 percent of our full potential. The Roman emperor Marcus Aurelius was one of those who exceeded that ten percent. Wouldn't it be wonderful if we could exceed that ten percent on the other end of the spectrum? The end that stands for peace, love, kindness, and goodness?

When Jesus and His apostles were caught in the storm on Lake Tiberius, I think Jesus probably knew of the perilous possibilities. But by taking the risk, He taught His apostles a most dramatic lesson in faith. He taught them that the "rock of ages" would see them through.

So if you have been in the harbor of inertia too long, why not venture out into the sea of life? Remember: "Nothing ventured—nothing gained"!

Changing of the Guard

From Babe Ruth to Reggie Jackson,

from penny loafers to work boots,

from Bing Crosby to Shaun Cassidy,

from real to artificial,

from senior prom to senior citizen,

from pompadour to receding hairline,

from Dixieland to disco,

from countryside to urban sprawl,

from carrier pigeon to TeleStar,

from George Washington to Watergate,

from arrows to A-bombs,

from cowboys to cads,

from Bibles to Belfast,

from "I do" to "I'll see,"

from get up to get down,

from church bell to boogie,

from too few to too many,

from the hope of 1776 to the bleak prediction of 1984—

the only thing constant is change, someone once said.

But there is One who never changes: Jesus Christ—

the same yesterday,

today, and forever.

Pinch Hitter

Baseball's experts have always acknowledged the difficulties of pinch-hitting. After sitting on the bench for hours and with little or no advance warning, the pinch hitter is called upon to enter the contest. With the game on the line, he must deliver or fail in only one try.

I had the pleasure of attending a game at Dodger Stadium. Late in the game, Manny Mota was called upon to "wave his magic wand." As he had done so many other times, he delivered. That hit made him the most productive pinch hitter in baseball history[1].

Upon hearing this announcement, we gave Manny a well-deserved standing ovation. Furthermore, the cheering would not cease and the game could not be resumed, until the Dodger hero came out of the dugout to doff his lid.

For years, the difficulty of being a substitute has been recognized. Whether you are a substitute teacher, preacher, or parent—keep on swinging. "The results of your good works follow you," Revelation 14:13 reminds us.

---

* Printed with permission of Los Angeles Dodgers Inc.

Whoops!

While walking home from the grocery store, something caught my eye. A two-handed lady was attempting to lug home three large grocery bags. Momentarily, one bag fell to the ground. The poor lady was trying to figure out what to do, when I happened upon her. She could not speak English, and I had no way of knowing how far away she lived.

Pressed for time, I held up one hand as a sign for her to wait. I ran back to the store and sped back with a shopping cart. After helping her load it up, I returned home. The incident had left an impression upon me.

At one time or another, we all try to carry a load that is too cumbersome. When this happens, there are alternatives.

We can try to streamline our lifestyle to allow us more time. We can buy time-saving devices; but often we may only replace the savings in time with another activity. We can ask for help. One of the three methods will help alleviate most situations. For more complex situations, try the methods in combination.

Is Life What We Make It?

I read recently—in a daily devotional, of all places—"Life is what we make it." Is it really?

Did any of us choose the locale or area of our birth? Were we given a choice of parents, siblings (if any), or many of our other relatives? Did you choose all the schools you've attended? Did you pick your own teachers? How many people are physically handicapped by choice? How many elect to have mentally handicapped children? Are all the elected officials the ones for whom you voted? Are the people who are in position of authority the ones you put there?

These people and circumstances often have far-reaching and long-lasting effects on our lives. I have seen good and intelligent people spend their lives in low-paying jobs. I have seen less worthy and less intelligent rise to exalted earthly positions.

Your answer to the next two questions will determine your answers to the preceding ones. While Jesus was hanging on the cross, was His life what He had made it? Did He get what He deserved here on earth?

Pretty People

Pretty people are easy to love;

their gift is obviously from above.

But what of those who were not blessed?

Can they be equal to the test?

Surface beauty fades and ebbs;

it can be a trap like spiders' webs.

When, at last, it's finally lost,

how does one escape the cost?

But if you have a sure foundation

built in advance, without reservation,

you will have the timeless charm

that father time can do no harm.

For when your mind's on earthly things,

like pots of gold and diamond rings,

you may miss out on a greater call,

and then, in the end, you'll lose it all.

Integrity

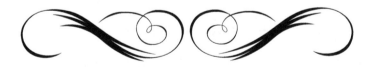

He Can Dream

Bo's youth group needed to raise funds for their annual project. It was decided that everyone in the group would go out and find aluminum cans. Not only would they bring in the needed money, but the looks of the community would improve. Each member was supposed to clear an entire field or a vacant lot. They were to meet together in four hours, with all their recyclable aluminum cans.

As Bo trudged through the field, he saw a nice shade from a tree. Bo sat down under it and fell asleep. As he slept, he began to dream. He dreamed that all the others had returned and missed him.

After counting their cans, they realized they were a little short of their goal. They set out in search of Bo and found him asleep on the job. They didn't say anything; they just stood and looked down at him.

The sound of a motor awakened Bo. He got up and diligently searched for field. Bo met the others, and the cans were counted. Not only had they reached their goal, but Bo won a prize for gathering the most cans.

Phantom Father

Steve was just about to leave work when his thoughts were interrupted by the sound of Joe's voice.

"Hey, Steve, how many kids do you have?"

"One," Steve responded.

"What's the matter? Don't you like kids?"

"Sure, I like them," Steve answered.

"Why don't you have more than one then?" Joe pressed.

"I am strongly in favor of population control, Joe."

"Well, I love kids. I have three and another one on the way. I work two, sometimes three, jobs to support them."

It was Steve's turn to ask a question. "When do you see your children, Joe?"

"Well, uh, uh, usually, I don't."

No!

About a year ago, I attended a social function that I will always remember. It was a dinner dance sponsored by the California Nurseryman's Association.

Before dinner was served, the president of the association asked one of the younger members to offer a prayer of thanks. To everyone's surprise, this otherwise pleasant young man refused. He told everyone that he did not want to pray to someone he did not believe in.

While most of the members were appalled, I admired the young man for his honesty. He could not pray from his heart; therefore, he refused to pray with his mouth. Placed in a similar situation, many people would have done otherwise.

Before any of us write this young man off as hopeless, let's recall a story that Jesus once told:

> "Now what do you think? There was once a man who had two sons. He went to the older one and said, 'Son, go and work in the vineyard today.' "I don't want to,' he answered, but later he changed his mind and went. Then the father went to the other son and said the same thing. 'Yes sir,'

he answered, but he did not go. Which one of the two did what his father wanted?"

"The older one," they answered. (Matt. 21:28–31)

A Hole in His Theory

The company president arrived at this office at 8:00 a.m. He immediately went over to the supervisor to check on the night crew's production. The crew came in at midnight, and they would all be going home in a half hour. The president noticed that there was still a noticeable amount of work to be accomplished. He inquired as to why the crew was cutting it so close.

The supervisor tried to assure him that the work would be completed on time.

Noticing a box of doughnuts and a pot of coffee on a nearby table, he replied, "Maybe if they didn't eat so many doughnuts and drink so much coffee, they would do a lot better."

After saying this, he went over to the table and helped himself to a doughnut. Then he indulged himself in a cup of coffee before retiring to his office for the day.

What! No Conscience?

Gary had been having a lot of trouble since he took over as manager of the apartments. Ralph, who wasn't even a tenant, was the source of most of the trouble. Since Ralph was not a tenant, Gary had asked him to stay away from the apartments. But as soon as one tenant would get tired of Ralph, the troublemaker would move in with someone else.

One afternoon, Gary was tidying up the pool area. He noticed a wallet, which belonged to Ralph. Gary saw there was no money in it and was reluctant to return it, face to face, to his antagonist. Gary put the wallet in a plastic bag and dropped it in a mailbox.

Several days later, Ralph was raising hell by the pool. Gary asked him to improve his behavior and was met with more disobedience.

Gary asked Ralph, "Did you get your wallet back?"

"Yeah, I figured it was you," Ralph said. This was, obviously, Ralph's substitute for thanks.

One night around midnight, Gary was awakened by a commotion. As usual, Ralph was present.

Gary asked him to quiet down; Ralph responded with a swinging fist. After dodging several punches, Gary wrestled Ralph to the ground and pinned him down. Ralph's face looked as big as a watermelon, but Gary stifled the urge to punch it.

The next day, Ralph said to Gary, "Hey, man, wasn't that a great fight we had last night?"

"What fight?" Gary answered. "I didn't even throw a punch at you."

Ralph laughed.

Having been sick for a week, Gary decided to go to bed. Gary thought he'd put the Do not Disturb sign on the door and sweat out his flu. Lying there, pouring with perspiration, Gary heard the doorbell.

I won't answer it, Gary thought to himself. After ten minutes of music, Gary changed his mind.

Who was at the door? You guessed it—Ralph. It seems Ralph's last friend had kicked him out, and now Ralph was asking Gary to intercede for him, with the irate tenant.

Gary refused and wondered if Ralph had any sense of shame or a conscience.

Hands Down

Henry, a fellow worker, explained his distress to me. He had developed a problem in one of his hands whereby much mobility was lost in the use of his fingers. He told me he had been to many doctors and had not achieved any satisfaction whatsoever.

Since I had experienced a similar problem, I directed him to a local orthopedic specialist. This particular doctor had given me almost instant relief, and within weeks, I had regained complete movement. Henry listened politely to my account, nodding approvingly from time to time.

Several months elapsed, and I asked him if he had been to my doctor. The answer was in the negative. Two years after our conversation, he still has not taken my advice. It is difficult to understand since his disability impairs his production at work and threatens to force him into an early retirement.

Sometimes, we are given spiritual advice which we refuse to explore. To do this habitually could cause disastrous consequences.

Jesus Christ

On a Clear and Starry Night

Jesus, I love you—

I know you've loved me from the start

Jesus, I love you—

I'm glad we'll never have to part

I love you so,

I know our love will grow and grow.

Then, someday, our love can reach the height

of a clear and starry night.

The night I met you,

the stars were shining up above.

That was the start

of our lasting love

Buy, Buy, Blues

The storefront sign caught the young man's attention. "Christian bookstore," it proclaimed.

Upon entering, he was greeted immediately by a middle-aged salesman. "How are you?" the salesman queried.

"How are you?" the young man returned his greeting.

"Fine, fine," replied the salesman. "What can I help you with, today? We have a complete line of albums, tapes, and cassettes."

"I don't have anything on which to play them," the young man answered.

"Well, how about some fine books? We have thousands of them."

"I already have a book," the younger man stated evenly.

"Maybe you'd like some of our latest bumper stickers?" the salesman ventured.

"I wouldn't be able to use them because I don't have a car," came the unexpected reply,

"How unusual!" the surprised salesman exclaimed. "Perhaps you'd like to buy some tickets for a forthcoming concert?"

"How much are the tickets?"

"Only ten dollars," the salesman responded pleasantly.

"I don't think I can afford to spend ten dollars for the concert."

"Say, what kind of Christian are you anyway?" the older man demanded.

"I am the Alpha and the Omega. I am the First and the Last. I am Jesus."

Listen, the Statue Spoke!

Mickey was taught to believe in Jesus since he had been a tiny boy. Mickey knew that Jesus saw everything he did and heard everything he said. The problem? He was terribly afraid of Jesus. He thought that Jesus was waiting to punish him, severely and instantly, for every mistake.

In Mickey's father's room, there was a statue of Jesus. Whenever Mickey went into that room, the statue made him extremely nervous; he couldn't wait to escape from its foreboding presence.

One night, the statue spoke to the troubled boy. "Mickey, do not be afraid of Me. I love you and want to protect you from harm. You are a good little boy, and you will go to heaven with God and His angels."

Mickey awoke, after a peaceful night's sleep. He went straight into his father's room and looked at the statue; no longer frightened, Mickey smiled. That night, the renewed child prayed, "I love you too, Jesus."

Role-Playing

Long before role-playing became popular, the Creator of all roles decided to try His hand at acting. He decided to play the part of a man. He played the part better than anyone before or since.

He began as all men begin—as a baby. Even at the usually rebellious age of twelve, He was obedient to his mother. To show poor people how to act, He grew up in a state of poverty. To show blue-collar workers how to conduct themselves, He worked as a carpenter. To set the example for ministers, He died without money.

Jesus

Oh my Jesus,

how I love you so (Jesus)!

Just can't let you go

'cause you make my heart feel all aglow.

And, sweet Jesus,

with your eyes that shine (Jesus),

won't you please be mine?

Love me past the end of time.

Burned Out at Thirty-Three

How many times have you heard phrases like "Slow down"; "Take it easy"; "What's the rush?"; "If you don't slow up, you'll burn yourself out?"

Jesus heard similar phrases, but He also heard God's voice leading Him on to accomplish what He was sent to do. Jesus always obeyed God's voice; He was obedient even unto death.

The apostle John, referring to Jesus, stated it thusly: "The Light shines in the darkness, and the darkness has never put it out" (John 1:5).

John, as usual, is right on target. The Light has changed only in form. The Light has made the transition from visible to semi-visible. His Light still shines.

Diff'rent Strokes

Long before the saying "Diff'rent strokes for diff'rent folks" became popular, a man named Jesus walked the earth. Although He was the Son of God, Jesus knew that different situations called for diverse methods. A study of Jesus's teachings and miracles will reveal a variety of strategies:

1. Jesus healed the Roman officer's servant, long distance. (Luke 7:1–10)

2. Jesus, awakened from sleep, still had the presence of mind to exercise power over the forces of nature. (Mark 4:38–39)

3. Jesus finds out the name of His adversary before taking action. (Mark 5:9)

4. Jesus is moved to act by the faith of a man's friends. (Luke 5:19–20)

5. Jesus heals, without being aware of it. (We may sometimes do likewise.) (Luke 8:44)

6. Jesus exercises His healing power, despite the objections of his detractors. (Luke 6:10)

7. Jesus heals amidst vicious and unfounded gossip. (Luke 11:14–15)

8. Jesus multiplies food for a hungry people. (Matt. 14:19–20)

9. Jesus changes His plans due to overwhelming circumstance (faith). (Matt. 15:21–29)

10. Jesus heals, after others have tried and failed. (Matt. 17:14–20)

11. Jesus uses plant life to dramatize a spiritual principle. (Matt. 21:19)

12. Jesus raises a dead man for his mother's sake. (Luke 7:14)

13. Jesus heals despite receiving only 10 percent of the thanks He deserves. (Luke 17:14–19)

14. Jesus heals an enemy. (Luke 22:50–51)

15. Jesus performs a miracle for the sake of a marriage celebration. (Marriage is holy and worthwhile in God's sight.) (John 2:1–11)

16. Jesus heals a man after the man had sought a healing in vain for thirty-eight years. (John 5:8)

17. Jesus risks death to bring a friend back from the dead. (John 11:1–44)

18. Jesus performs a miracle, as a reminder of a previous miracle. (John 21:6)

19. Jesus allows Peter to defy the laws of nature. (Matt. 14:29)

20. When His enemies set a trap for Him, Jesus springs the trap on them. (Matt. 22:15–22)

21. On one occasion, Jesus had to get physical. (Matt. 26:39)

22. About to be handed over to death, Jesus prayed the ultimate prayer. (Matt. 26:39)

23. To prepare for his monumental ministry, Jesus fasted. (Matt. 4:2)

24. When the devil tried to tempt Him out of context scripture, He defeated him with scripture used in its proper context. (Matt. 4:7–11)

25. Jesus bowed to His parent's wishes. (Luke 2:48–52)

26. He associated with sinners, when He deemed it necessary. (Matt. 9:10–13)

27. He had to arbitrate childish disputes. (Matt. 20:20–28)

28. He had to correct a boastful friend. (Matt. 26:33–34)

29. He refused to accept help in the form of violence. (Matt. 26:51–54)

30. He allowed His services (as Redeemer) to be sold for a mere thirty pieces of silver—much less than He is worth. (Matt. 26:14–16)

When facing various circumstances, we should use a suitable stroke. In so doing, like the apostle Paul, we may become "all things to all people."

Persuasive Perceptions?

Two men saw Jesus covered with sweat and blood. As He staggered under the weight of His cross, they approached Him.

"Hey, man, how's it going? How are you feeling today?"

"Not so well, at the moment," He responded.

"Aw, wadda ya mean? The world's a wonderful place, full of beautiful people. Think positive—look on the bright side of things."

"If it is as you say, I may as well lay down My cross and forget about going back up to Heaven," Jesus answered.

Fortunately for us all, Jesus did not see the world as others saw it (Mark 8:34).

The Human Side of Jesus

For some time, while I understood that Jesus was God, I did not fully understand that He was also a human being. This was a precarious position for me to be in. Without the knowledge of Christ's humanity, I could not fully realize the staggering price that was paid for my salvation.

God chose to send Jesus in the form of a human being. God could have chosen to reveal Him to us in some other form. It is important to us, as Christians, to understand Christ's humanity; for in understanding His humanity, we may better understand our own.

During the thirty-three years that Jesus walked on the earth in human form, He ran the gamut of human emotions, feelings, and experiences. May I share some of them with you?

1. He was exposed to the elements. (Mark 1:13)

2. He felt the pangs of hunger. (Matt. 4:2)

3. Jesus was tempted. (Matt. 4:1)

4. At least one of His potential followers was prejudiced against Him. (John 1:46)

5. His sanity was questioned—by his own family, no less! (Matt. 3)

6. At times, He was tired, thirsty, angry, ignored, joyful, saddened, ridiculed, humiliated and physically abused, and pain was heaped

upon Him. (Matt. 8:24; John 4:7; John 2:15; Luke 7:46; Matt. 11:25; Mark 5:40; Mark 15:19)

7. He was filled with sorrow. (Matt. 26:38)

8. Jesus had financial pressure applied to Him. (Matt. 17:24)

9. He felt a need for His body to be cared for. (Mark 6:14)

10. He was betrayed by someone close to Him. (Mark 14:44)

11. He felt a deep sense of loneliness. (Mark 15:34)

12. He went through physical death. (Mark 15:37)

13. Above all these, He was filled with love. It was this divine sense of love that made Him tell us (after his resurrection), "Because I live, you also will live." (John 11:36)

Love

God's Overwhelming Love

As I thumbed through my wallet, I stopped to admire some photographs of the two girls dearest to me—my wife and our daughter. As I gazed upon them, I felt my heart grow warm. I was so filled with a feeling of love for them that my eyes filled with tears.

In that moment, I received an inkling of the immensity of God's love for us. Although the full scope of His love for us is beyond human comprehension, I appreciated the "look through a glass darkly" moment.

The Sign of Love

The sign of love

shows up through the haze

of money-mad

and thinly clad

people in a daze,

adoring stones of jade.

Its Light is strong,

and its song is sweet.

You won't go wrong—

don't avoid its heat.

Just let yourself be free;

you'll be you and I'll be me

Its sound is loud,

but unlike a crowd,

it doesn't have to wade

through all the fools and fakes.

You can see on any street,

and they're frozen with defeat

Love is happiness;

though you may have less

than other people have,

feel the softness of its salve,

like the smoothness of a dove.

Can you make the sign of love?

The Power of Love

I would like to share with you the results of a little girl's love for kittens.

Some years ago, Rhonda used to visit her grandparents on Sunday afternoons. While visiting, she noticed a cat in the window of the neighbor's mobile home. Although shy, she went over and introduced herself; she then asked if she could come in and play with their cat. Rhonda started spending so much time visiting the neighbor's cat that her parents would have to collect her next door when it was time to depart.

During one of these collections, they were invited inside also. A warm friendship, including five people and a cat, developed.

After a time, Rhonda's father asked Bob, the cat's owner, for advice on how to overcome a negative attitude. Bob advised him to read some books by Norman Vincent Peale.

After reading an armful, Rhonda's father realized that Dr. Peale was getting much of his material right from the Bible. The girl's father decided to go straight to the source and soon became an avid reader, attended church regularly, became an usher, a Sunday school teacher, and a committed Christian writer.

Yes, the writer of this story is proud to be the father of Rhonda. I never stop marveling at the result of my little girl's love for kittens.

Is It Worth It?

Our daughter's year-old kitten, Sugar, really enjoys getting love. In an effort to receive our physical affection, she often gets underfoot. She considers the joy of getting love worth the pain of being trod upon.

Although some pain is usually involved, to give and receive love is a privilege. Is the privilege of giving and receiving love worth the pain? Jesus thought so!

Clem's Climb

I first met Clem at work.

During our coffee break, he had the attention of many as he told them how he used to "roll drinks" on Friday nights. To the uninitiated, Clem explained that since—for most people—Friday was payday, he and his former teenage friends would gather outside a local bar. They would wait 'til someone came out who had obviously had too much to drink, and they would take his money from him. If he offered any resistance, he would be forcefully subdued.

One Friday night, these young men relieved a man of five hundred dollars in the manner. The following morning, while Clem was at the grocery store, he noticed the victim of the previous night. The victim had his children with him, and Clem could hear him refusing their every request. Since the man had been relieved of all his cash, he was desperately trying to keep food costs to a bare minimum. The man did not recognize Clem as one of his assailants for he had been too drunk and it had been dark.

Clem told the man he was one of the ones who had taken his money the night before. Clem's share was two hundred dollars, which he promptly returned to the man. In addition to this, Clem promised to deliver the other three hundred to him as soon as possible—even if he had to get a job and earn it.

This took much courage on Clem's part. Since he was not alone, the man might have overpowered him or pressed charges against him.

Upon hearing this story, I immediately thought of the words of Jesus: "The great love she has shown, proves that her many sins are forgiven" (Luke 7:47).

About a month after hearing this story, I was reading my Bible during my lunch break when Clem approached me. He asked me why I was always reading it.

I told him that I needed the comfort and guidance that it had to offer.

He then said to me, "What about the bad parts?"

I asked him what bad parts he was referring to.

"Like when Pilate 'put the finger' on Jesus," he said. "But it was Jesus's own people that did it [instigated by the religious leaders]." He then told me that he still thought it was terrible that Jesus was put to death.

I explained to Clem that it was all within the will of God and that all we had to do to be saved was to believe in Jesus.

He then surprised me with the following statement: "I believe in the Dude, man."

Most of us would probably have said "Praise God" or "Amen"; but however we say it, what really matters is that we do believe. Jesus said, "He who believes in Me will not be put to shame" (Rom. 10:11).

Well, I don't believe Clem will be put to shame for he is now a reader of the Bible. The other day, my heart soured as his friends started making fun of him for reading the Bible. My heart soared because I heard Clem's courage shine through as he answered them, "If you guys are too foolish to read the Bible, don't put me down for reading it."

I am happy to report to you all that this story is being written and submitted with the full knowledge and permission of Clem. He did not even ask me to use a fictitious name. I will always be grateful for having known Clem and for the graphic lessons in courage and love that he has taught me.

I will close with the words of the apostle Paul: "But the greatest gift of all, is the gift of love" (1 Cor. 13).

Recipe for Reverence

Many grams of gratitude,

sixteen ounces of honesty,

one pound of piety,

a flagon of faith,

an ear of endurance,

a pat of patience,

one platter of praise,

three spoonfuls of sincerity,

one heap of helpfulness

stirred into action,

two cupfuls of kindness

shaken into service,

add the leaven of love,

an armload of awe—

make the best feast

you ever saw.

Adios, Amigo

Jose was the oldest man in the plant; he was also number 1 on the seniority list. Most of his coworkers resented his seniority; they hoped he would retire soon, so they could move up on the list.

While Jose was on annual leave, word was received that he had been admitted to the local hospital. Rod decided to visit him.

"You're the only one from the plant who has come to visit me. I'm sure glad you came." Although Jose tried to display a cheerful exterior, there was pain deep in his eyes.

When Rod rose to depart, the old man extended a gnarled hand. Rod shook it gently.

"Adios, amigo." Jose smiled.

"Adios to you, my friend," Rod responded.

The following week, the news of Jose's death was all over the plant. All but one expressed their "heartfelt" sorrow. The one who refrained was Rod.

Isolation Booth

A game show popularized the idea of an isolation booth. The purpose of the booth was to help the contestant think more clearly and to block out the noise of the crowd (and their incorrect answers).

Jesus commanded us to "love one another" (Matt. 19:19). This command is sometimes difficult to follow. When people behave in a manner that goes against our grain, it is difficult to love them. But if we can isolate the deed from the person, we increase our chances of achieving the goal that Christ set for us.

In the field of medicine, it is sometimes necessary to amputate a part of the body to save a life. If such a drastic measure as this can, utilized successfully, then surely we can isolate a person's deeds from their souls (eternal lives). By doing this, we may help to save them (as well as ourselves).

Miscellaneous

Paradox of a Former Existence

While driving my Cadillac,

people looked and said, "Is that a fact?"

They didn't know it was just an act

I had accidentally signed a pact,

giving up my chance for happiness.

Then I knew how it felt

to be all alone,

with no friends to phone,

in a timeless zone,

like an unheard tone.

Well, I wore fine clothes;

I had rows and rows

of fine threads.

But what good were they

'cause I had to pay

with a fake pose?

Yeah, when I was oh so young,

I didn't know the value of an iron lung.

All the wrong songs were being sung;

all the wrong folks were being hung.

But it's turnabout day,

and now they're hangin' me.

Then I knew how it felt

to be almost gone,

skinny and forlorn,

full of thorns and scorn,

like a broken bone.

Well, I had to hide my name

'cause I felt ashamed

to hear it said.

When a good person looked at me,

I had to hang my head.

I was really down and out;

yeah, there wasn't any doubt.

It didn't do no good to pout

'cause I followed the wrong route.

I was ready, then, ready to concede.

Then I knew how it felt

to be disappearing,

no one really hearing

what I could no longer hide—

my invisible pride.

Yes, I finally cried.

Commentary on "Paradox of a Former Existence"

In "Paradox of a Former Existence," I was focusing on hypocrisy—mainly my own—and how it seemed to pervade my life some years ago. I felt that I had taken some wrong turns on the road of life by embracing superfluous values. However, since I lived in a society that seemed to value hedonism and materialism, I felt that I was (to some extent) a victim of what seemed to me to be the established order of things.

At the same time I was condemning myself, I was also indicting the society that had shown me false values. I felt, and still feel, that the priorities of the world have become so twisted, jumbled, and warped that it may be impossible to ever straighten them out.

To give a more specific example, the other day, as I was leaving work, one of the ladies jokingly (?) referred to me as a traitor because I was not going to prostitute myself for two hours of overtime pay. I wanted, instead, to send time with my daughter.

In my usual serious manner, I told her, "I cannot be a traitor, as long as I am true to myself."

The Shell

The shell is what's left over

when sadness hangs and hovers,

when all you see is troubles

and they all come in doubles (the shell).

You might say I'm on a trip,

but that's because you think you're hip.

Don't show me any of your needles;

I've already seen too many evils (the shell).

I'm a shell, you're a shell,

everybody is a shell

'cause the less you show, the less you lose—

listen to me all you fools (and tell).

Tell me how you're all so cool

when you can't even see the rules.

You're as wrong as the outsiders,

even though you say that you're not fighters (tell).

Tell me all about your flowers

and how you stole your stolen hours.

You say you gotta climb our hill,

but first you know you gotta fill (your shell).

He Who Does Not Gather

Fred was really enjoying his newfound freedom as owner of his own business, after years of working for someone else.

One day, shortly after opening, one of Fred's customers invited him to church. Fred politely declined. He was already short on time because of his hew business. Besides, getting involved in church would take away from his family time and his golf game.

Fred found himself devoting more and more time to his business and a diminishing amount of time with his family. The inevitable breakup of the family ensued.

In an effort to fill the void left by his departing family, Fred started to drink quite heavily. His drinking eventually led to his failure in business. Now bankrupt, Fred could never spend any money on golf. So Fred lost his three most important priorities—his business, his family, his hobby.

One day, while passing a church, Fred heard a preacher's voice boom from inside: "He who is not with me is against me, and he who does not gather with me scatters" (Matt. 12:30).

Fred decided to go inside; after all, he had plenty of time now.

Indians Are In

Indians are "in" this—

in antipollution ads, they shed a tear

because the land has been defaced,

the damage done is not erased.

Noble red man or savage red beast?

No better than some, no worse at the least.

Whenever we hear of two extremes,

the truth is usually in between.

For a sum of money, they sold Manhattan;

their sheets are certainly not satin.

First, destroy their buffalo meat

then wear moccasins on your feet.

Because white man spoke with forked tongue,

Red man's at bottom on social rung.

When again what conquered band

was ever given back some land?

Only red men can grow peyote;

it can be found among coyote.

Maybe soon the conquerors will pout—

Indians are in, and we are out.

Circle of Influence

It is a fact that every one of us are included in a circle of influence. The things we say and do affect those around us; the things others say and do can affect us. If I tell you it's a wet, miserable day, you will tend to agree without thinking. If you tell me it's a wet, miserable day, I will tell you I am thankful for the rain. When I tell you this, you will at least stop to think.

Even Jesus's ministry was affected by those around him. We are told in Mathew 13:58 that He did not do many mighty works there because of the people's unbelief. In Luke 13:31–33, Jesus intended to be in a certain area for three days. However, because Herod sought to kill him, He left sooner than He had planned. He was not afraid to die, but He had to fulfill everything what scriptures said about Him by dying at the right time and in the right manner.

Because He was obedient to the point of shedding His innocent blood for us, His circle of influence now includes about one billion.

Hats Off?

A college instructor complained to me, "The use of symbolism in western movies is a form of racism—e.g., the use of white hats represent 'good guys' and the use of black hats to portray 'bad guys.'"

In the Bible, there are symbolic references to white clothes as "the good deeds of God's people." The darkness or things that belong in the dark is likewise representative of evil. To my knowledge, no one has yet accused the inspired writers of the Bible of racism.

Therefore, I conclude, to suggest that the use of black and white hats in movies is a form of racism is without foundation. Furthermore, it is this type of extrapolation that promotes mistrust among people.

Suicide!

For a long time, Oscar had been contemplating suicide. His main problem was which method to choose. Since he would no longer need his car, he decided to use it to accomplish his secret plan.

That night, he pulled onto the two-lane highway. It was a pretty lonely stretch. After about five minutes, he saw the headlights coming toward him. He gripped the steering wheel as tightly as he could and braced himself for the inevitable.

Unfortunately, the family in the other car was not braced nor did they want to die.

Music

Musical Memories

In spite of warnings from a few religious leaders, I have been a fan of rock and roll music since its inception. While there may be some validity in the warnings, it must be noted that many rock and roll songs contain a positive religious message. For an exercise in research or just for listening pleasure, recall this partial list of oldies but goldies:

- "There but for Fortune" by Joan Baez
- "Three Bells" by Browns
- "Scarlet Ribbons" by Browns
- "Tall Oak Tree" by Dorsey Burnette
- "Turn, Turn, Turn" by Byrds
- "The Other Man's Grass" by Petula Clark
- "Your Own Backyard" by Dion
- "Reach Out of the Darkness" by Friend & Lover
- "You'll Never Walk Alone" by Gerry & Pacemakers
- "Day by Day" by Godspell
- "Spirit in the Sky" by Norman Greenbaum
- "My Sweet Lord" by George Harrison
- "Oh Happy Day!" by Edwin Hawkins Singers

- "Jesus Christ Superstar" by Murray Head

- "A Satisfied Mind" by Bobby Hebb

- "Michael" by Highwaymen

- "The Wings of a Dove" by Ferlin Husky

- "I Believe" by Lettermen

- "Home of the Brave" by Jody Miller

- "Put Your Hand in the Hand" by Ocean

- "Crying in the Chapel" by Elvis Presley

- "I Don't Know How to Love Him" by Helen Reddy

- "Jesus Is a Soul Man" by Lawrence Reynolds

- "Look to Your Soul" by Johnny Rivers

- "Think His Name" by Johnny Rivers

- "He" by Righteous Brothers

- "Tell It All Brother" Kenny Rogers & First Edition

- "My True Love" by Jack Scott

- "I'll Never Find Another You" by Seekers

- "Games People Play" by Joe South

- "Don't It Make You Want to Go Home?" by Joe South

- "Walk a Mile in My Shoes" by Joe South

- "Mr. Businessman" by Ray Stevens

- "Everything Is Beautiful" by Ray Stevens

- "You've Got a Friend" by James Taylor

- "Billy and Sue" by BJ Thomas

- "Mighty Clouds of Joy" by BJ Thomas

- "Woman Helping Man" by Vogues

- "Lean on Me" by Bill Withers

Nature

Back to Nature

So you're going back to nature
that's encouraging to see
hiking, health foods, soft hair
and a little less TV.

Cultivate an organic garden,
DDT can beg your pardon.
Watching birds arranged in trees
helps make future memories.

In a forest, wet and green,
feast your eyes upon the scene,
as it was in the beginning,
stops your dizzy head from spinning.

Sit beside a sparkling stream,
as you weave your favorite dram,
where the waters ebb and flow,
hear the angels' trumpet blow.

You've grown tired of the superficial,

so you're making it official.

Give the Creator an approving nod,

and for nature, please thank God.

The Bush

A couple of years ago, I felt somewhat like a rock in the center of a seesaw, tottering back and forth, between giving my heart to the Lord and keeping it to myself. I was on the brink but lacking the crucial impetus, many times.

One day, after hiking to a waterfall in the mountains (I love nature), I was inexplicably driven to my knees at the base of the waterfall. On both sides of me, sheer cliffs rose up about fifty feet. Even though I had never seen a tumbleweed in that area before, as I knelt down and prayed, a tumbleweed appeared directly above me (between the two cliffs).

Defying the laws of gravity, it hovered above me for a full minute or two. At the conclusion of my prayer, it descended at my feet. I was totally overwhelmed by the experience, and like Moses at the burning bush, I knew that I had been in the presence of the Lord.

Therefore, at the age of thirty-two, I decided to be baptized (even though I had been baptized as an infant). Since then, I have saturated myself with the Bible and have become an usher and Sunday school teacher.

Sunday is now the high point of my week. (I used to dread Sunday sermons, etc.) To my amazement, I was chosen to serve on the church's commission for Christian education, and our pastor even invited me to preach the sermon a couple of times.

I am thankful for all of the encouragement given to me by the members of our church and my own family. And I am filled with gratitude to my almighty Creator, who would turn my love of nature into an everlasting spiritual experience.

Spirit of the Sea

Our Creator's liquid largess,

I hope we won't make it a mess.

Full of beauty and fish,

imbibe as much as you wish.

The source of many a painting,

'tis a shame that we are tainting.

Storms blamed for the loss of hand,

less damage at sea than on land.

By the strength of its waves,

it hammers and hollows out caves.

By the consistency of its tides,

we're able to go for boat rides.

And speaking of salty ol' surf,

imagine swimming on turf!

Good advice for you and for me—

let's all thank God for the sea!

Negativity

Refocus

Tony and Walter worked for the same employer. Over a period of several months, the two men had dozens of conversations. Their dialogue was almost always the same.

"Boy, Walter, that guy Marvin sure is getting on my nerves. He sure has a big mouth."

"You'd better refocus on your thoughts, Tony. Someday you'll do something drastic."

"That's easy for you to say, Walter, but . . . "

Tony had a particularly bad day at work. He walked outside to be greeted by sweltering weather. As he started to get in his car, he noticed that one of his tires was flat. As he was changing it, Marvin walked up to him.

"What's the matter, Tony? Did someone let the air out of your tire? Ha-ha!"

"Yes, and it was probably you."

As the words were flying out of his mouth, Tony's lug wrench crashed down on Marvin's skull.

Tony is now serving a prison sentence for committing manslaughter. I wonder what he's focusing his thoughts on now.

Smillin' Seth

Seth was a pretty nice fellow. Although basically happy, sometimes he would let little things in life get him down. I would like to share some of his experiences with you. Perhaps you may find some solutions to his problems.

Seth smiled happily to himself; in another hour, he would get off work and spend the weekend with his family. Seth really loved his family. With only one hour to go until quitting time, Seth decided to take it easy and maybe have a quick look at this favorite magazine.

He had just opened the magazine when Mr. Green, his boss, walked into the office. Mr. Green looked sternly at Seth and told him he didn't appreciate anyone reading magazines on company time. Seth put the magazine aside and resumed his clerical duties.

"Everybody else does it," he mumbled. "Why do I always get caught?" Seth tried to forget the matter, but Mr. Green's stern-looking face kept creeping back into his thoughts.

It was while Seth was driving home that he almost got into an accident. He was driving along, thinking about Mr. Green, when another driver suddenly cut in front of him. Seth slammed on his brake just in the nick of time. He was pretty sure that the man had deliberately tried to upset him. Seth promised himself that he would not become upset over the near collision.

While Seth was busy thinking about not becoming upset, he didn't notice how unusually blue the sky was that day. He didn't even notice the snow on the mountains placed there last night.

Finally, Seth arrived home. His children, excited by the prospects of being off school for the day, waved their pretty drawings in the air for their father to enjoy. Seth didn't really see them for he was already explaining the injustices of the day to his pretty wife, Donna. He launched into his complaint without even greeting his family with the hugs and kisses they'd been hoping for.

After changing into his "grubbies," Seth went outside to work in the yard.

"Ouch!" Seth yelled, as he stepped on something sharp.

Seth was pretty sure that his bleeding foot was somehow related to the uncomplimentary thoughts he'd been having about Mr. Green. He dashed into the house for a Band-Aid. After a futile search, Seth called out do Donna. "Why don't we have any Band-Aids around here?"

Donna responded pleasantly, "You said the kids were wasting them on minor cuts and that I shouldn't buy anymore."

Seth was getting exasperated. "Why did you have to listen to me?" was all he could say.

After a relatively uneventful evening, the alarm went off, and Seth turned it off.

"It can't be Sunday morning already," he said, and then he went back to sleep.

Half an hour later, he was awakened by Donna's soft voice. "You'd better hurry, honey, or we'll be late for church."

Seth raced through his shower and threw on his clothes.

After backing the car out of the garage, Seth looked at this watch and noticed they were running late. Because of this, Seth ran through a traffic signal a few seconds after it had turned red. Half a block later, Seth pulled over in front of the policemen's flashing lights.

"I'm sorry, sir," the officer said. "You failed to stop for the last signal, and I'm afraid I'll have to issue you a citation."

On the rest of the way to church, Seth bemoaned the fact that the "fuzz" weren't spending enough time chasing real criminals.

By the time Seth and his family got to church, the sermon was over. After the service, Seth asked the clergyman what the sermon was about. "It was about the need for a positive attitude, Seth."

Seth breathed a sigh of relief. "Oh well, I'm glad I didn't miss much," he stated. "If there's one thing I've got, it's a positive attitude."

Complaints, Complaints!

"You wouldn't believe the day I had yesterday," Shirley began.

Leon braced himself for the coming spiel.

"My next-door neighbor kept me on the phone for an hour and a half. When I went to get my hair done, my regular hairdresser was on vacation. I had to settle for a substitute! Can you imagine that?"

As the two continued to sort letters, Leon taped one over his offended ear. Shirley did not notice the poor man's attempt to stem her tirade.

"I forgot my thermos and had to buy coffee out of the machine. It didn't even give me a full cup. I spoke to Benjamin when I came in, and he hardly answered me. I wish he weren't so quiet. It really gets on my nerves. Did I tell you I'm pregnant, and I don't even know who's to blame? This place really brings me down. Why! For a nickel, I'd go home sick."

Leon walked over to Shirley as he reached into his pocket. "Here's a dollar, Shirley. I'll see you in twenty days."

All Wet

Due to the prolonged drought, the bodies of many animals lay strewn across the wilderness. Many times, clouds would form; but, as if to tease the thirsty beasts, they did not deliver what they promised. There were almost no waterholes left, and the unfortunate creatures that remained were getting desperate. If rain did not come soon, none would survive.

Late one autumn, the teasing clouds began their customary formation. One cloud became angry with another, and the two collided; their contents burst forth. The other clouds immediately followed suit.

Down below, the alert critters pricked up their ears. As soon as they realized what was happening, they leaped joyously and thankfully into the air.

But one old beast sulked under a tree. "I don't see why they're all so glad. My beautiful fur is getting all wet!"

Obedience

Not a Cheat Skate

Danny really enjoyed his new skateboard. His dad had given it to him for his birthday. He also received all the skateboarding accessories. The boy's father cautioned his son to use the protective equipment whenever riding.

Danny's friends dared him to ride down a big hill without his helmet and pads. Not wanting to be called a chicken, the boy accepted their challenge. The result was a broken arm.

Although his arm healed quickly, the boy's father began to work overtime in an effort to fulfill his financial obligations. After an especially long day at work, the boy's father arrived home quite tired.

"Hey, Danny, how about mowing the lawn for me this evening? I could sure use your help."

"But, Dad," the boy replied, "I wanted to go skateboarding this evening. Can't I ever have any fun?"

Where's Your Proof?

In Luke 5:12–14, we read,

> Once Jesus was in a town where there was a man who was suffering from a dreaded disease. When he saw Jesus, he threw himself down and begged Him: "Sir, if you want to, you can make me clean!"
>
> Jesus reached out and touched him. "I do want to," he answered. "Be clean." At once the disease left the man. Jesus ordered him, "Don't tell anyone, but go straight to the priest and let him examine you; then to prove to everyone that you are cured, offer the sacrifice as Moses ordered."

As proof of his healing, the man was to offer the sacrifice that Moses had commanded. Likewise, to prove to everyone that we are healed (saved), we should also offer the sacrifice that Moses ordered. We should keep the commandments.

Enjoying Life

One night's indiscretion had resulted in an unwanted pregnancy for Becky; and she became a mother while still in high school. Unable to support herself, or her baby, Becky remained at home with her parents. Her parents had worked hard for many years to raise their children; now, they had another responsibility to bear.

While watering the front lawn, the unwed mother heard the roar of a motorcycle. She smiled pleasantly at its rider, and he screeched to a halt.

That evening, Becky asked per parents, "Will you watch the baby tonight? I met a young man this afternoon, and he asked me to go out with him."

Her responsibility-ridden parents replied, "We're pretty tired and we'd appreciate it if you would watch your own baby."

The girl mumbled, sullenly, "Don't you want me to enjoy life a little?"

Stamp Out Selfishness

Teddy had always considered his father, Chuck, to be his pal. Today, Teddy's pal was taking him for a rare treat. Several months ago, Teddy had started a stamp collection. Chuck was taking his son across town to pick out some of his favorite stamps. After spending all he could afford, Chuck took his boy to lunch.

After lunch, Teddy asked if they could go back to the stamp store. The boy's father reminded him that he had already spent enough. The boy pleaded for another two dollars' worth.

"Well, if you promise not to say anything to your mom about it . . . "

When the two pals arrived home, they sat down to a big dinner. After they had eaten, Chuck suggested that Teddy help with the dishes.

Teddy rebelled. "But, Dad, I'm tired from shopping."

Chuck insisted that Teddy help, or there would be a punishment.

Teddy whispered to his dad, "If you punish me, I'll tell Mom that you spent more than you were supposed to on my stamps."

Not wanting a confrontation with his spouse, Chuck conceded. Teddy was glad to have gotten off so easily.

Years later, as Teddy looked over his stamp collection, he remembered the shameful way he had treated his father. His guilt-ridden conscience told Teddy that he had not really gotten off so easily.

What If?

Today, we live in an age of games—word games, chase games, financial games, and athletic games—of every variety. In keeping with this trend toward games, I am going to play a game using some characters in the Bible as markers. The name of the game is What If?

What if Matthew had decided that his job as tax collector was more important than following Jesus? We would all be missing an important version of the Gospel.

What if Noah had not followed God's instructions by building the ark? The history of the human race might have ended some seven thousand years ago.

What if the people whom Jesus healed during his earthly ministry had no faith in Him? Would they have been healed?

What if Judas had enough faith to repent after he betrayed our Lord? Would he have been forgiven? I think so.

What if Peter, like Judas, had committed suicide after denying Jesus? Instead, he asked for forgiveness with many tears (and received it!).

What if the men guarding the tomb of Jesus had not accepted a bribe? What if, instead of saying that the apostles had removed the body of Jesus while they were asleep, they had told the glorious truth of his resurrection?

What if Jesus had not interceded for the woman caught in the act of adultery? What chance would she have had of withstanding the unyielding stones hurled by unyielding hearts?

What if David had thought he was too young to fight Goliath?

What if Moses had thought he was too old to lead God's people out of slavery and bondage? Moses was eighty years old when God used him.

What if Jesus had become tired of the pain and sorrow of the cross? What if he came down from it and destroyed all His enemies? He could have done that, if He had not submitted to His Father's will. But then the scriptures would not have been fulfilled and we would still be lost in our sins and suffering under who knows what delusions.

I do not have to limit myself to these biblical examples. Just last night, I wondered if I would really attempt to write this article. What if I had not? I don't know the answer to that question, but I do know this: the blood of Jesus Christ is too precious to play games with.

And now, it is time for me to include some of you in this game. What if some of you think that churchgoing is primarily a social affair and that reading the Bible is mostly an intellectual exercise? What if you think you need more proof before making a heartfelt commitment? Then I say to you, we already have all the proof we need—right in the Bible.

What if you would like to become a wholehearted follower of Jesus Christ but you're not quite ready?

What if you would like to rededicate your life to God today but are waiting for a better time?

My friend, what if you never get another chance?

It's a Dog's Life

No, this is not a story about the poor quality of life. It is a story about how all living things are intricately connected.

Jan read the new role on the office's bulletin board. "If they think I'm going to stop drinking coffee at my desk, they're crazy!"

She promptly went to the coffee machine and purchased a cup of the dark liquid. She made herself comfortable at her desk and reached for a quick sip. Preoccupied with her work, she knocked the cup over and stained some outgoing mail.

The next day, the irate postal patron stormed into the postmaster's office.

"Which one of clumsy clerks spilled his coffee on my mail? This envelope contained an important document, and now it's ruined."

The postmaster was upset at the unwarranted accusation. Coupled with other (possibly unjust) complaints, the harried postal official went home in a gloomy frame of mind.

It didn't take long for him to upset his poor wife. He, in turn, was unjustly harsh with her son. Greg, bewildered by his mistreatment, retaliated by kicking his dog. The unfortunate animal ran blindly into the street and was run over.

Hearing Greg's remorseful cries brought his neighbor Jan out of her house.

"What's wrong, Greg?" she queried.

"My dog just got killed by a car!" he wailed.

Not realizing her part in the series of misfortunes, she quickly blurted her response, "Oh! Some people are so careless, if only they would follow the rules!"

The Reluctant Neighbor

Jan knew that she was supposed to be home by ten o'clock, but she was having so much fun at the fair. Her father had told her that it was dangerous to walk home late at night.

When the teenage girl started for home, it was about eleven thirty. A few blocks from home, a car pulled up alongside her. A young man jumped out and grabbed her.

When Jan began resisting him, the man became angry and began to hit her in the face. She managed to break free and fled to the nearest house.

Steve was awakened by the incessant ringing of his doorbell; he looked at the clock, and it registered midnight. A young girl dressed in white shorts stood on his front porch.

Through the locked screen door, the girl told him her story and asked him to drive her home. Wary of the possibilities, Steve suggested that she use his phone to call her parents. The girl said that her family had no telephone. Steve doubted that anyone in their suburban community lacked a telephone. He then suggested that the police come for her. The girl refused and left as quickly as she had arrived.

That afternoon, as Steve was mowing his lawn, a truck stopped in front of his house. A big, burly man jumped out and demanded to know why he had not honored the request of a damsel in distress. Steve told the man about the questionable lack of a telephone. The man was surprised and admitted that his daughter had lied about the telephone.

He then apologized to Steve for his gruff manner and intimated that perhaps his daughter had learned a hard but valuable lesson. Steve was pretty sure that the man was correct.

Let's Ditch

Scott and Rick were good friends. Lately, they had spent so much time with each other, they had neglected their schoolwork. As they walked to school together, they told each other how bad their score would be on today's English exam. Suddenly, Rick got as idea.

"Hey, Scott, let's ditch school today. We'll be off the hook, as far as the English test goes. Then we'll study real hard for our finals."

Scott readily agreed, and the two youths looked forward to a day of fun. They played pinball machines, ate junk food, and saw a movie. Each laughed to the other about how they had gotten out of taking the English test.

They arrived at their respective homes about the time they would normally get home from school. Rick's mother asked her son how he'd done on the English test.

"Okay, I guess," he answered.

A similar conversation was taking place at Scott's house.

That evening, Judy, a friend of Rick's mother, called. During the course of the conversation between the two ladies, Judy happened to mention how nice Rick's hair looked that day. One word led to another, and before long, Scott and Rick's secret was out.

Before the evening ended, Scott and Rick had promised their parents that they would never skip classes again.

The next morning in English class, Rick and Scott were dumbfounded to hear their teacher say, "Everyone clear your desks for the test. I'm sorry I couldn't give it to you yesterday, but I was home, sick."

God/Good—Devil/Evil

It is obvious, from the title, that the word *good* is derived from *God*; the word *evil* is a derivative of *devil*. But let's see what a closer look reveals.

In order to arrive at *good*, a letter is added to *God*; to arrive at *evil*, a letter is subtracted from *devil*. Likewise, God adds to our happiness; the devil subtracts from it. Therefore, if we follow God's ways, He will increase our happiness. If we follow the devil's ways, we jeopardize our own chances for eternal happiness.

Jailbreak

Merv was serving the last year of a three-year sentence. Prison life was intolerable, and he wished that his last year would fly. Although he had only ten months to go, Merv decided to cast his lot with four other inmates who were planning an escape.

During the escape, two of the men were stopped by bullets. Merv and two others made it over the wall, but within a week they were apprehended and returned to their former residence.

The intolerable ten months' remainder is now an unbearable five years ten months.

Inward Baptism

It is not the outward ceremony of baptism that saves us; rather, it is the inward change that we undergo that is more important. It can be likened to the old belief that outward circumcision was "salvation insurance." It must also be remembered that when the Pharisees came to John the Baptist, he sharply rebuked them. He did this because he knew that the Pharisees would not submit to being "washed on the inside."

There is a built-in resistance to obedience. When we begin to overcome that resistance, our baptism begins to produce the proper fruit.

Remember, a person can be saved in the water or in the desert!

A Day without God

Glen was in his early forties and had been yearning for more freedom. He was tired of responsibilities and obligations. Glen wished that, for just one day, he (and everyone else) could be totally free—i.e., a holiday from God. He vowed that the next day would be the day and greatly looked forward to it.

However, before the next day had ended, Glen's children had disobeyed his every command; his brother was murdered and Glen's neighbor (who had accepted a bribe) swore that the saw Glen pull the trigger; Glen's house was broken into and robbed by someone else who was totally free; and Glen caught his wife in the very act of adultery.

Now that his free day was over, Glen wished that everything could revert itself . . . unfortunately, it cannot.

Out-CB'd

Chuck smiled to himself as he drove along. "Now that I have my new CB radio, I don't have to obey the speed limits anymore."

To prove his point, he edged his speedometer past the seventy mark. If "Smokey" was around, he would be notified by some "good buddy."

Sure enough, before "Smokey" could close in on him, Chuck was tipped off. To escape prosecution, he turned onto a seldom used road. After traveling a mile or so on his alternate route, Chuck chuckled to himself. "Hot dog, fooled 'em again!"

Then, out of nowhere, a "fly in the sky" descended. Finding his path blocked by the helicopter, the "communications expert" spun his truck around.

"I'll just go back the way I came," Chuck snorted. But the police car that he had so skillfully avoided blocked that means of escape too.

Chuck slammed on the brake and jumped out of his truck. "Hi, good buddies!" was his embarrassed greeting.

The Ten Loopholes

1. There is only one God—except for the one that can be seen in your mirror.

2. Do not use God's name in vain—unless you're at work or in your motor vehicle.

3. Remember the Lord—unless you're too busy.

4. Honor your parents—unless they are stepparents.

5. Do not kill—unless you're angry or there is something to be gained by it.

6. Do not commit adultery—unless you get the chance.

7. Do not steal—unless you can do it without getting caught.

8. Do not lie—unless it will make you look good.

9. Do not covet someone's spouse—unless they're wealthier or better looking.

10. Do not covet anyone's good, deeds, or ideas—unless they're newer, better, or smarter respectively.

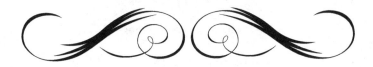

Overcoming Temptation

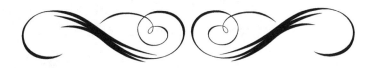

Jesus through and Through!

Here's a song for all ages,

to renew all your pages—

there is Jesus in me;

there is Jesus in you.

When you're tempted to hate me

for things that I do—

remember, Jesus in me,

think of Jesus in you.

When you're tempted to rob

'cause your treasures are few—

dwell on Jesus in me,

feed on Jesus in you.

If you're inclined to blame

or to call me a name—

don't forget Jesus loves me,

don't forget Jesus loves you.

Should your future seem dim

and your plans all fail through—

there's still Jesus in me,

thanks for Jesus in you.

Patience

A Basket Case

The apostle Paul will always be remembered for his courage in the face of danger. He fearlessly faced many dangers in order to spread the Gospel. However, in Acts 9:25, Paul literally became "a basket case"; the famous missionary had to be hidden in a basket in order to escape death in Damascus.

In an effort to live a life in keeping with the Gospel, we too may find times when discretions is indeed the better part of valor. During these occasions, we must keep in mind that God does have plans for us. In order to achieve those plans, however, we may have to bide our time.

The Disposable Society
Shortcut to Nowhere

Denise was nursed on canned formula and wore only disposable diapers. As she grew into childhood, she was fed instant meals on paper plates. The girl's mother remarried several times; so the girl received instant fathers, brothers, sisters, and other relatives, from time to time. Frequent moves made her an instant member of a new school and a new neighborhood.

When Denise turned sixteen, she received a brand-new automobile. Friends gave her pills so that she was able to change her moods to go up or down, whenever she desired. Upon high school graduation, the girl with the push-button lifestyle was given a position with her current father's firm.

Denise met Randy, and it was love at first sight. For wedding presents, the newlyweds received every material item imaginable. Among other things, they were given a new home, completely furnished.

After six months of maladjustment, Denise obtained . . . you guessed it—a quickie divorce.

Hit and Run

After forty years of palatial luxury, Moses decided to see how the other half lived. When he saw the Jews (his people) being mistreated, he decided to take matters into his own hands by murdering one of their antagonists. Moses realized that his deed had been detected; he also realized that his intercession was rejected. Moses then fled to a remote region where he spent the next forty years in relative obscurity.

When, at the age of eighty years old, the Lord decided to make Moses a leader; he showed his hard-won humility by demurring; Moses expressed inadequacy for the task due to his inability as speaker (something none of our current leaders would dare admit).

After receiving God's counsel, Moses led his people out of bondage. He performed many unprecedented miracles during his years of leadership. Moses gave the credit for his success to his Creator, humbling himself before Him.

I would like to sum up his life with a verse of scripture from The Living Bible:

> Don't be impatient of r the Lord to act!
> Keep traveling steadily along His pathway
> and in due season He will honor you with

every blessing, and you will see the wicked

destroyed. (Ps. 37:34)

I'd Be Happy, if Only . . .

In Philippians 4:11, Paul boldly states, "I have learned in whatsoever state I am in, therewith to be content." Paul's proclamation of faith is in direct contrast to the title of this article. Many of us have begun conversations, similar to the title of this article.

If you are feeling unhappy due to the rain, try to imagine what life on earth would be like without water. If the intensity of the sun's rays is wilting you, remember that some people live and work in the desert (some without benefit of air-conditioning). If the lack of money or material things has you down, think of those who have less. If physical afflictions cause you pain, pray for other whose afflictions are worse. If old age is wearing you down, remember those who are older than you (there are some). When career prospects seem bleak, remember those in the unemployment line. If there is a communication problem between you and a member of your family, remember those without families or anyone else with which to communicate; you may even remember times of loneliness yourself. When lack of time frays your nerves, think of those who have nothing but time on their hands (due to disability, among other things, etc.)

As you can see, there is a mental antidote for many maladies. For those maladies not mentioned, an antidote can be obtained form the greatest Physician/Psychologist of them all. His supply is endless.

Let It Germinate

It is human nature to expect the fruits of our labor to bloom instantaneously. "One good turn deserves another," as the saying goes; but our turn doesn't always come right away. When we sow our seeds of good deeds, we must sometimes wait for them to germinate. Nature teaches us many valuable lessons: a baby, consummated in love, does not make its appearance for nearly a year!

Jesus knew the importance of the germination period. He gave this parable to reveal an important truth:

> The Kingdom of Heaven is like this: A man takes a mustard seed and sows in his field. It is the smallest of all seeds; but when it grows up, it is the biggest of all plants. It becomes a tree, so that birds come and make their nests in its branches. (Matt. 13:31–32)

Let's Hear It for Slow Growth

In an age where time is of the essence and time-saving devices have become a necessity, we Christians would love to have instant spiritual maturity. Such expectations, however, are unrealistic. There are at least two reasons why we must mature slowly:

1. If we were to achieve instant spiritual maturity, what would we have to look forward to here on earth?
2. It is through our own slow, and sometimes painful, growth that we learn to be patient and understanding with others in their areas of weakness.

In Luke 17:5, the apostles said to Jesus, "Make our faith greater." The Lord told them that if they had faith even as small as a mustard seed (one of the smallest of seeds) that it would grow to large proportions. This parable is a perfect example of the eventual effectiveness of slow growth.

Perseverance

Chippin' Away

One day, I wanted to purchase a cup of coffee from a vending machine. The only money I had was a five-dollar bill. After a ten-minute search, I was able to trade it for five singles. I started to insert one to of the singles in the dollar-bill changer, but it was out of change.

The next phase of my hunt saw me receive two fifty-cent pieces for a dollar bill. The coffee machine took only nickels, dimes, and quarters. At last, just before my lunchtime was over, I managed to exchange one of the fifty-cent pieces for two quarters.

Sometimes, we could like to solve a problem or situation all in one swoop; sometimes, this is not possible. But if you can divide the problem in half and maybe cut a half in half again, you're on the road to a solution.

So if something's got you bugged, just keep chippin' away.

Hidden Truth

Yesterday, while working diligently, I was surprised to hear the voice of Johann behind me. The custodian, a Christian, told me that (in his opinion) I did more work more accurately than anyone employed there. I was left slightly amused by the remark.

That evening, I wondered why, after thirteen years on the job, my boss, a non-Christian, had not observed me in the same light Johann had seen me in.

While reading the Bible, I believe I received the unexpected answer in Matthew 13:14–15:

> This people will listen and listen, but not understand; they will look and look, but not see. Because their minds are dull, and they have stopped up their ears and have closed their eyes. Otherwise, their eyes would see, their ears would hear; their minds would understand; and they would turn to me, says God, and I would heal them.

What about Him?

As Christians, it is sometimes difficult to endure hardship while others around us seem to prosper.

When Jesus revealed to Peter that he would be crucified like his Master, Peter looked at John and said, "'Lord, what about this man?' Jesus answered him 'If I want him to live until I come, what is that to you? Follow me!'" (John 21:21–22).

When Jesus's teachings became too difficult for some of His disciples to comprehend, they protested. Jesus answered, "Does this make you want to give up?" (John 6:61).

It has always been human nature to question God's purposes. But if we can say with sincerity "Thy will be done on earth, as it is in Heaven," we are on the road to peace of mind here on earth and eternal life in heaven.

The Maniac

After an all-too-brief two-day honeymoon, Larry reluctantly reported back to work.

Upon entering the building, he was greeted by a white-faced supervisor. The supervisor stammered, "Wh-what are you doing here?"

"I am scheduled to work tonight," Larry answered.

"But, but I thought you were dead," the supervisor stuttered.

"What are you talking about?" Larry asked with surprise.

"The maniac told us that you and your wife were killed in an automobile accident on your way back from Las Vegas."

The maniac had discovered a new device for gaining attention.

Larry calmly strode to his case and began to sort letters; such goings-on were not uncommon there.

The maniac had worked hard to earn his nickname. During his career in the post office, he had thrown a chair at a man, nearly decapitating him; hit a man in the face while the man's hands were held behind him; for the ladies, he only stuck his tongue out at them and threw eggs at their cars; and in the supposed privacy of the men's lounge, the maniac would remove his shirt in order to admire his physique.

Once, he knocked a man out of his seat, as a dozen or so people watched the proceedings. Larry volunteered to be a witness but was told that enough witnesses had already been obtained. A week later, the case was dismissed due to a lack of witnesses.

Bewildered by all this, Larry surmised that everyone was simply afraid of the maniac.

The following day, the maniac rushed toward Larry, tearing off his shirt. "So you wanted to be a witness against me? Tomorrow I'll bring my gun and kill you. Remember, I can withstand anything."

Larry went to the postmaster and reported the threat made against his life since it was a federal offense to threaten the life of a federal employee. The postmaster, not wanting any blemishes on his administrative record, figured that the best defense was a tough offense.

"You are less than nothing in my sight," he told Larry. "If you pursue this matter any further, I will see to it that it costs your job."

Larry knew that the postmaster would, one way or another, make good on his threat. Larry had a decision to make. Larry would have to risk his life going forward for the sake of his family's security. Larry was so upset over the series of events that he sought advice from an older and wiser Christian friend. The friend advised him to quietly persevere.

During the ensuing three years, Larry endured more threats and more violent behavior.

Finally, the postmaster died of a heart attack, his heart wearied by protecting his record.

Shortly after that, the maniac discovered something that he finally could not withstand—he succumbed to cancer.

Upon receiving the news, Larry went to his case and began to sort letters. He had quietly persevered.

Spiritual Gardening

We read this in the Bible:

> Then Jesus told them this parable: "There was once a man who had a fig tree growing in his vineyard. He went looking for figs on it but found none. Lo he said to his gardener, 'Look, for three years I have been coming here looking for figs on this tree, and I haven't found any. Cut it down! Why should it go on using up the soil?' But the gardener answered, 'Leave it alone, sir, just one more year, I will dig around it and put in some fertilizer. The if the tree bears figs next year, so much the better; if not, when you can have it cut down.'"
>
> (Luke 13:6–9)

As God's people, we are expected to bear fruit. There will be times when people will dig into us with words or deeds. There will be times when so much fertilizer is placed around us that life will seem to stink!

If we are able to look upon such digging and fertilizing as agents of growth, we will surely rise above our circumstances. The culmination of our growth will result in the production of much fruit—the kind of fruit that God is looking for among us, His trees.

Paragon of Perseverance

Life is not always fair. In a large government-controlled industrial plant, there is a very conscientious custodian. Though this man works harder than anyone on the custodial staff, he is only allowed to work six months of the year. For several years, this gentleman has missed out on all fringe benefits and half of his potential salary. Red tape has kept him in this state, while many sluggards have been placed on the full-time payroll.

When I asked him about this situation, I expected a bitter reply. Instead, he smiled and told me how thankful he was to have a wife and a home. He told me that he even manages to feed many of the stray cats in his neighborhood. I commended him for his perseverance and positive attitude.

As I returned to work, I heard him sweeping and whistling. He may be near the bottom of the industrial ladder, but he's tops in my book.

Twelve Perfect Ones

In May 1959, Harvey Haddix Jr. accomplished what no one, before or since, has ever come close to duplicating. For twelve innings of major league baseball, Harvey pitched a perfect game—i.e., he allowed the opposing team *no runs, no walks,* nor did his team commit any errors. In other words, no opposing player reached first base.

In the thirteenth inning, Harvey lost his perfect, no-hitter, shutout game . . . all on one hit. The defeat was the most difficult one of his career; absorbing it made him overflow with tears. To see a professional athlete cry is an unforgettable experience.

Yet Harvey lived to pitch again and win again. Although he has not been selected to the Baseball Hall of Fame, he has been nominated.

When we lose a tough one, let's remember Harvey Haddix.

Your Enemies Make You Strong

To desire everyone to be your friend could be a foolish fancy. Many times, it is your enemies who make you strong. The sharpness of your enemies' hatred hones your wits. Prayer comes often when you are surrounded by detractors. Working among antagonism, at close quarters, helps you develop patience and endurance—all priceless virtues.

No matter how many enemies plot against you, there is one overpowering Friend.

The Crow's Nest

An old-time sailing vessel's highest point was its crow's nest. From this vantage point, one could see things in much better perspectives than at lower levels. An additional advantage of being in the crow's nest was that waves washing over the deck could not sweep you overboard to a watery grave.

Applying this principle to our spiritual lives, we can climb into our own crow's nest when the daily news and soap operas of life overwhelm us. How do we reach this crow's nest? It can be done in a variety of ways: prayer, church attendance, and Bible reading . . . to name a few.

I would like to share with you some of the waves (1978 style) that the crow's nest principle helped my family and I withstand last year:

January passed by without much trouble and then February. I had a painful bout with a kidney stone, followed by surgery on both feet. While recovering at home, my wife came in crying because the neighbors' children had thrown rocks at her while she was watering the lawn. One of the rocks found its mark on her polio-stricken leg, thereby ending her irrigational efforts for the day. Unable to do anything about the situation, I prayed for my wife and the neighbors and their children.

Later that night, I was awakened by a commotion in front of our house. It seems a man was exercising the gears in his transmission by running back and forth over our trash cans. He continued this until the containers could no longer serve their purpose. Again, unable to walk, I prayed for the man. (The trash cans were beyond help.)

Then came spring. A succession of domestic misfortunes almost left us unsprung.

Our new, thirteen-month-old car developed some problems, a month after its warrant expired. I came home from work to find our central heating and air-conditioning roof unit on fire. The damage done left it beyond repair, and the entire unit had to be replaced. The next morning, my Sunday school students ran over to me and asked me to sponsor them in a bowling tournament. I didn't have the cost, but I told them I'd see what I could do. I skipped breakfast and lunch for a week, and the following Sunday I was able to answer their request.

And then the water heater had to be replaced. A serious plumbing problem ensued. The garage door opener would not function. The stereo had to have major work. Our television set died, despite the operations of a "skillful surgeon." The washing machine broke, and the dryer had to be repaired on the same day.

Summer came, and I got a week's vacation from my job, but a close friend needed surgery and asked me to fill in for a week to keep her from losing her business. I didn't mind filling in, for the battle with the appliances had left me without vacation money. I celebrated my birthday by taking my wife to the hospital. She had fallen and hurt her susceptible foot and was unable to walk for a week. This was followed by two roof leaks.

Five days before Christmas, I missed four days of work because of the flu (despite a precautionary flu shot). During those four days, the refrigerator went out. I spent New Year's Eve at home, recovering from another foot surgery.

Do all this make me want to give up on God and His Kingdom? No! Instead, we thank Him for His blessings. (There were some.) We also know that others suffered worse losses than we did (some irreplaceable). We prayed that 1979 and the succeeding years would be a little kinder to us.

Already, there had been some good signs. After sheltering two homeless friends for two years, they found a place of their own. This left us with more elbow room and less financial stain. Our neighbors had a new baby. The addition to their family made their house too small, and they have moved. I sincerely hope their parental efforts bear better fruit than their previous efforts bore.

We look forward to seeing all of you in the ultimate crow's nest—heaven!

The Longest Mile

The year was 1962. Our country was in the midst of what has become known as the Cuban Missile Crisis. Clayton enlisted in the United States Air Force and looked forward to serving this country.

After several weeks in basic training, Clayton developed a foot problem, which necessitated surgery. The doctor wrote out a three-day duty excuse and had someone help the young man to his barracks.

Clayton had just settled into his bunk when the training instructor entered the room. The sergeant asked Clayton why he was in bed. Clayton explained and showed him the duty excuse.

The instructor tore it up, threw it on the floor, and told Clayton to put his boots on and come downstairs.

Clayton, barely able to lace up his boots, came outside. There, the sergeant confronted him.

"Does your foot hurt you pretty bad?"

"Yes, sir," Clayton answered.

The sergeant looked Clayton in the eyes and asked, "What would you do if I jump on it?"

Clayton knew that either an honorable or dishonorable discharge would hinge on his answer. He knew that his reply would probably be a physical reflex reaction aimed in the sergeant's direction. Clayton prayed that this would not be necessary.

The sergeant, apparently satisfied by Clayton's silence, decided that his authority had been asserted in front of everyone and ordered Clayton into formation with the others.

The march to the dining hall was one mile. Clayton thought, *If he asks you to go one mile, go with him two miles.*

Still numb from the anesthetic, Clayton hardly felt anything during his forced march. However, on the way back, his foot was throbbing, and he limped noticeably.

That night, as Clayton tossed in his sleep, he dreamed. He dreamed that he was called to the base commander's office. The general told him that someone had reported Clayton's antagonist to him. The general asked Clayton if he would like to have the sergeant court-martialed.

Clayton had a decision to make. The sergeant had quite a few years toward retirement. The sergeant had a wife and three children. Clayton looked at the stars on the general's shoulders. "No," he answered. The next morning, Clayton felt a little better.

Four years later, Clayton held the honorable discharge in his hand. He look at the piece of paper and wondered if it had been worth the trouble. It was the foot surgery and other similar incidents that had given him a dim view of military life in particular and life in general.

However, when bad memories assailed him, he opened the floodgates of his mind and let the words of the Bible come pouring through: "But if you endure suffering even when you have done right, God will bless you for it" (1 Pet. 2:20). Clayton had to agree that Peter is right.

Bunt

In the game of baseball, even the greatest hitters experience batting slumps. Slumps are prolonged periods of failing to get a hit. The more experienced hitters, while in the midst of a slump, will attempt to bunt in an effort to reach first base.

In the art of bunting, the hitter merely makes contact with the ball. After the psychological lift of getting a hit, the player will many times go on a prolonged hitting binge (much to his delight and to the delight of his fans and teammates).

As a writer, I have experience slumps; some have lasted as long as a week. One of the methods I employ to end my slump is to write a spiritually oriented poem. My pen is making contact with paper, and my mind is making contact with the Creator of all things. Our Creator is able to open up new avenues of thought for us.

The art of bunting is not just for baseball players and writers. I believe it can be applied to many professions and situations. All you have to do is relax and make contact.

Deep Roots

Since you have accepted Christ Jesus as
Lord, live in union with Him. Keep your
roots deep in Him, build your lives on
Him, and become stronger in your faith,
as you were taught. And be filled with
thanksgiving. (Col. 2:6–7)

In the preceding New Testament nugget, the key word is *deep*. A study of nature shows us that the strongest trees have the deepest roots. It is this depth of root system which enables trees to withstand times of tempest and days of drought. In the depths of the earth, roots find water.

If we keep Christ's words (the Living Water) deep in our hearts, we will not wither away to a state of spiritual drought. Neither will we be blown away by winds of change nor stormy sieges.

Are You a Hero or a Villain?

Do you sometimes find yourself cast into certain roles? Sometimes a hero and sometimes a villain? When you hit a home run to win the game, it is hero time. When you have to discipline a child, you may feel like the villain. These feelings are real, and we all experience them at one time or another.

While Jesus was driving the merchants from the temple, He probably appeared to be a villain. When He raised Lazarus from the dead, it was hero time again. Regardless of His appearance, Jesus was the Son of God. He knew that He would join His Father in Heaven when His earthly stay was over.

If we have this same knowledge, the "hero versus villain" syndrome will not cause us to fall victim to an identity crisis.

Earned or Unearned?

In the game of baseball, all runs scored by the opposition are charged against the pitcher. The pitchers have one consolation, however.

If the opposing team scored its runs due to his teammates' fielding flaws, the runs are put into the "unearned run" column. This keeps his earned run average low. Since a pitcher negotiates his contract on the basis of his earned run average, this is important to him.

In the game of life, charges are often aimed at us. Sometimes, the charges are valid (earned); sometimes, the accusations are unjustified (unearned). St. Peter has some words of wisdom for us on this subject:

> My dear friends, do not be surprised at the
> painful test you are suffering, as though
> something unusual were happening to
> you. Rather, be glad that you are sharing
> in Christ's sufferings, so that you may
> be full of joy when His glory is revealed.
> Happy are you if you are insulted because
> you are Christ's followers; this means that
> the glorious Spirit, the Spirit of God is
> resting won you. If any of you suffers,

it must not be because his is a murderer or a thief or a criminal or meddles in others people's affairs. However, if you suffer because you are a Christian, don't be ashamed of it, but thank God that you bear Christ's name.

The time has come for judgment to begin, and god's own people are the first to be judged. If it starts with us, how will it end with those who do not believe the Good News from God? As the Scripture says, "It is difficult for good people to be saved; what then will become of godless sinners?" So then, those who suffer because it is God's will for them, should by their good actions trust themselves completely to their Creator, who always keeps His promise. (1 Pet. 4:12–19)

Temple under Construction

Have you ever wondered why you are sometimes surveyed surreptitiously? Were you surprised to find your pillars punished aside by bulldozers? Has your family tree ever been uprooted and transplanted? Was your lot ever regarded in order to give you a new slant?

Have misfortunes floored you? Have your walls ever crumbled all around you? Did it cause you to blow a fuse, the ceiling, or the roof? Did your favorite team finish in the cellar? Did you ever get your spiritual wires crossed? Were you shocked or cross?

Did the doctor ever tell you that your favorite drink was rusting your pipes? Did you ask him to pipe down? Remember when your utility bills were just gas? Did you every have to listen to a phony on your phone? Has the Department of Sanitation every "blown your cover"? Have you ever found yourself with a full house when you were planning on keeping a poker face?

Is the condition of your driveway driving you bananas? Is your pool draining you of your resources? Have you ever felt akin to your doormat? Have you had to curb your temper because of your curbside mailbox? Have your eaves been dropping lately? Is there too little room in your rooms? Is there too much din in you den?

If you cannot insulate yourself from all of the aforementioned indignities, dig this:

> You, too, are built upon the foundation laid by the apostles and prophets, the cornerstone being Christ Jesus Himself. He is the One who holds the whole building together and makes it grow into a sacred temple dedicated to the Lord. In union with Him, you too are being built together with all the others into a place where God lives through His Spirit. (Eph. 2:20–22)

Pollutions

"Ssssh!"

Surrounded by excessive noise,

it's difficult to keep your poise.

How is it possible to concentrate

while the wall around you reverberate?

Isn't something quite the matter

when there's constant buzz and chatter?

Piped-in hourly news

will surly result in the blues.

There's never been a riot

in the stillness nor in quiet.

How's it possible to commune

while absorbing an endless tune?

An unending parade of activity

will blot out creativity.

My hearing ability grows lower

after an assault by a power mower.

Try to hear the song of a lark

while unattended doggies bark.

Read this poem real fast

before the next sonic blast!

Perils of Pollution

We're all making restitution

for accumulative pollution.

After all, cosmetology

took precedence over ecology.

We backpack in search of nature

while being victimized by legislature.

Our water's not fit to drink—

watch it corrode your sink.

To breathe a breath of air

is a gamble and a dare.

Sitting in a smoke-filled room

is a surefire way to doom.

Surrounded by trash and litter

is one way to grow bitter.

Tot our waste and refuse away on a barge

while population numbers grow too large.

Popularity

Crowd-Pleasers

The temptation to please the crowd has always been a very difficult one to resist. Several characters in the Bible were victimized by this temptation, when their desire to go along with the crowd became greater than their desire to do right.

When King Herod had the choice of setting free John the Baptist or beheading him, he chose the latter. Although King Herod enjoyed listening to John speak, John's words stirred up Herod's guilt. Guilt and fear are cousins; they can only be held in abeyance for so long. Guilt and fear wait for the right circumstances and then respond—usually, inappropriately.

For Herod, the circumstances were a combination of alcohol, sensuality, and the pride of being surrounded by famous guests. It was mainly for the sake of the crowd that John was murdered.

While the apostle Peter warmed himself by a fire, his presence was detected by a servant girl. The girl accused Peter of being a follower of Jesus. Since Jesus was an unpopular man at that moment, Peter denied knowing Him; before the night was over, Peter regretted the denial with many tears.

In private, Nicodemus acknowledged the wisdom of Jesus by seeking advice from Him. He even attempted to defend Jesus publicly. Today, he is identified with the Pharisees, his peers. The Pharisees, as a group, were persecutors of Jesus.

Try to picture the two thieves being crucified on either side of Jesus. As the crowd hurled insults at Jesus, one thief did likewise. What was his motive? Could he have lashed out at Jesus in order to obtain some degree of popularity for himself, perhaps even his release?

While one thief's motives are questionable, the motives of the other thief are unquestionable. He wanted to be in heaven with God. Due to the divine mercy of Jesus, that is where he now resides.

Mayhap the most notorious crowd-pleaser of all time was Pilate. Although Pilate believed that Jesus was innocent, he succumbed to the pressures of the crowd by whipping Jesus and then handing Him over to be crucified.

Anyone for going along with the crowd? Count me out!

Population Control

Fuel for Thought

Chris was filled with pride because his sixth son had just been born. He was hoping for three more so he could have his own baseball team. On his way home from the hospital, Chris noticed that his fuel gauge registered nearly empty. He quickly pulled into a station to tank up.

Ward was looking forward to camping out with his wife and child that weekend. In preparation, he drove into a service station, and only one other customer was there.

As Ward was filling his tank, he observed that the other customer seemed to be glaring at him.

"Is anything wrong?" Ward asked in a friendly manner.

"You'd better believe it, man! It's guys like you who are causing this energy crisis, you and your big camper."

Ward responded firmly, "Listen, friend, I did my bit for the energy problem by having only one child."

Chris quickly displayed his ignorance by asking, "What has that got to do with anything?"

Praise

The Mummy

When it is the night before payday and you are stationed at an air force base in Japan, you go to the base theater for an inexpensive evening of entertainment.

One particular evening, even the thirty-five-cent admission price did not seem like much of a bargain. Twenty minutes into the film, most of us were falling asleep. We were rudely awakened by the shut of "Mums, mums!"

No, we had not been attacked by a bunch of giant flowers; instead, an overenthusiastic viewer had burst with excitement at the overdue appearance of "the mummy."

The sight of someone walking around in grave clothes would surprise anyone. Once before, in real life, a man named Lazarus walked out of a tomb where he was similarly arrayed.

The one responsible for this miracle was not a movie director. None other than Jesus was the responsible party. People were so overcome that they ran ahead of Him, with palm fronds, and they praised God's greatness. May we do likewise on Palm Sunday and on all other days.

A Choir

The song is to a choir,

as a child is to its sire—

like a telegram to its wire,

or an airplane to a flier.

When you're really feeling low,

hear their lilting voices flow—

whether upbeat or more mellow,

all together or in solo.

If you're feeling all forlorn,

come and listen Sunday morn.

If you've suffered words of scorn,

feel the music being born.

Their sweet melodious praise

keeps me going on for days,

and while heathens walk in haze,

I am warmed by their arrays.

Tho' outside be rain or sleet,

we are warmed by vocal heat.

Like a bowl of fortified wheat,

they can lift you when you're beat.

When they sing that final note,

I am all prepared to float

like a sailor in his boat—

on their talent, I just dote.

As they weave their musical ministry,

I am transfixed by their wizardry.

How they synchronize trajectory,

it'll remain an unsolved mystery.

Prayer

Horse's Tale

With eighteen major fires burning simultaneously, it was difficult to remember to pray about all of them. Our family chose to single out the nearest one. It was in the northern section of Claremont, California, known as Padua Hills.

There was a large riding stable there, and we had enjoyed some excellent evening horseback rides. We would stet out at dusk. The trail wound through a beautiful forest, complete with a stream. For the return trip, we had to trust the horses to follow the trail for it would be totally dark by then. Upon returning, we were treated to a good, old-fashioned cookout. All this was now in jeopardy.

Do our prayers sound selfish to you? Perhaps. But it's funny how things work out. Immediately after the fire was extinguished, some acreage near the stable was earmarked for the construction of a Christian school. We have been looking for just such a school in our area. Much to our delight, our daughter will begin attending it next year.

(Scriptural Reference: Rom. 8:26)

Is Anyone Out There Listening?

To answer the question contained in this title, I will tell you a story.

It began last summer. Our pastor asked me to formulate and preach a sermon. After several weeks of contemplation, I didn't even have a title for a sermon. Finally, this came to me: "And you shall know the truth and the truth shall make you free" (John 8:32).

I felt I could speak for twenty minutes on the subject of truth, the truths that are contained in the Bible. After listening to a tape of my sermon, our pastor called Saturday evening and asked me to deliver the real thing in tomorrow evening's service.

On Sunday afternoon, I had the impulse to call and invite an old friend of mine to the evening service. I stifled the impulse for two reasons: He had never attended my church for he fellowshipped at a church ten miles nearer his home. I also did not want to appear to be seeking glory for myself. Despite these reasons, the urge to call him would not leave me.

Finally, I prayed, "Heavenly Father, if you want Keith to be at this evening's service, I know you are capable of arranging it Yourself."

About an hour before I had to leave for church, the doorbell rang. There stood my friend Keith, his wife, and his daughter. I invited them inside and told them the story. We all agreed that their appearance at my house was more than a coincidence because we had not seen or communicated with one another within the past six months. My conclusion? God hears and answers our prayers!

Witness

Many times during our earthly stay, we will want to witness for Jesus. Sometimes, our witness will have noticeable effect; sometimes, it will not. In the latter instances, we should not become discouraged.

To be rejected is not an enjoyable experience. Since Jesus was rejected, then we will be rejected at times also. It is natural for us, as Christians, to feel the burden for someone else's soul. Whenever we feel this burden, we should pray to God about it. Only God has the power of salvation in His hands. To have less power and influence than God is no disgrace.

Pray Always

"Pray always" is one of Paul's most remembered admonitions. I often wondered why he believed in always praying. To some extent, we are all products of our experiences. What experience caused Paul to believe in praying always? One of his adventures can be found in Acts 16:22–40.

After their undeserved treatment, Paul and Silas did not sit and bemoan their misfortunes; they sang hymns and prayed in the presence of other prisoners. The answer to their prayers came in the form of a violent earthquake. The earthquake released everyone from their bonds and opened the door.

When the jailer drew his sword in order to kill himself, Paul saved his life by letting him know that he and the other prisoners were still there. Paul knew that the jailer would have to pay for escaped prisoners with his own life. Instead of letting his oppressor die, he saved his life!

Amazed by Paul's selfless actions, the jailer then allowed Paul to help him and his family onto the road of salvation.

Most of us will never have an experience like Paul's; however, when we experience oppression in any form, let's remember to pray always.

Leaders Need Prayer

It has become fashionable to bemoan our political leadership and to downgrade the leaders of the world. I have even caught myself falling into this trap. Although our leadership sometimes seems inadequate, the Bible has some very specific advice to offer us on this subject:

> First of all, then, I urge that petitions, prayers, requests, and thanksgivings be offered to God for all people; for kings and all others who are in authority, that we may live a quiet and peaceful life with all reverence toward God and with proper conduct. This is good and it pleases God our Savior, who wants everyone to be saved and to come to know the truth. (1 Tim 2:1–4)

Pride and Vanity

Just a Closer Jog with Thee

A parody of the beloved old hymn will be presented in the form of a news bulletin update:

While the fun and benefits of exercise are to be given recognition, let's remember—no matter how fast or how far we run, we cannot run away from God.

By strengthening heart muscles, jogging may prolong our earthly lives. But when our earthly lives have finally ended, we will have to face God. He is the designer of all muscles, and no one is stronger than He.

Muscles Malone

"Muscles" Malone was extremely proud of is physique. He worked out with weights, machines, etc., eight hours every day. Some of his other hours were spent in front of a mirror, admiring what he had accomplished. Several of his friends had invited him to fellowship in their respective churches, but Muscles declined their offers of goodwill.

One day, Muscles attempted to break his personal weightlifting record. As his body quivered, he felt dizzy, and something wet was running down his chest. It was blood. He had overextended himself, and a blood vessel in his neck had burst. Surprisingly, there was no telephone in the gym.

The next day, when I walked in and found him dead, I remembered an appropriate verse of scripture:

> Physical exercise has some value; but
> spiritual exercise is valuable in every
> way, because it promises life both for the
> present and for the future. (1 Tim. 4:8)

He Left Them Cold

Harry was very proud of his attendance record. In eighteen years, he had never used a day of sick leave. Although he caught his share of colds and flu, Harry would never call in sick.

Whenever he became sick, his fellow employees would follow suit; it may have been coincidence. Whenever anyone suggested that here could be a correlation between his colds and theirs, Harry would laugh and accuse them of lacking in faith. As a result of his perfect attendance record, he came to be known as "Harry Hale."

During one Christmas season, Harry was forced to check into the hospital with a case of pneumonia. His perfect attendance record was shattered. During his lengthy recovery period, Harry began to reevaluate his concept of faith.

Dressed to Kill

Elizabeth was looking forward to making her annual Easter appearance at her local church. In preparation for the occasion, she went on an all-day shopping spree. After getting her hair and nails done, she purchased a new dress and new shoes, with matching handbag.

On Sunday morning, Elizabeth spent much time primping. Her rings, necklace, bracelet, and watch were chosen and matched with extraordinary care; makeup was applied flawlessly.

While admiring the reflection of the finished product, the telephone rang.

"Hello, Elizabeth?" the voice on the other end questioned.

"Yes, this is she," came her reply.

"This is Irene. Why didn't you come and pick me up for church this morning? I was looking forward to going with you."

Elizabeth glanced at the watch. "I didn't realize it was so late. Oh well, since it's lunchtime, let's go to Francesca's for cocktails. Anyway, the only reason all those people probably go to church is just to show off their new clothes."

His Yoke Is Easy

Tim and Tony shared the same employer.

One day, Tim got into a disagreement with the boss. Although Tim felt he was definitely in the right, he conceded his point. That evening, while reading his Bible, Tim came across Matthew 11:28–30:

"Come to me, all of you who are tired from

carrying heavy loads, and I will give you

rest. Take my yoke and put it on you, land

learn from me, because I am gentle and

humble in spirit; and you will find rest.

For the yoke I will give you is easy, and

the load I will put on you is light."

Tim was glad he had conceded to his boss.

The following morning, Tim sensed that his boss was in a bad mood. Tim went to Tony and shared the golden nugget of scripture that he had unearthed the night before. Tony was not interested in hearing about it.

Later, that afternoon, Tony became embroiled in a heated argument with the boss. One word sparked another, and in a flash of anger, Tony was left unemployed. Tony's yoke is not easy, and the burden of caring for his family is not light.

Immediate Gratification

For some, living in the now generation means immediate gratification in all areas of life. It is a sign of maturity, when a person is willing to forego immediate gains for the sake of future fulfillment. While many would argue against this theory, let's examine two cases in point.

Helen takes a lot of pride in her appearance. Most of her days revolve around the shopping center. Armed with credit cards, she pyramids their unpaid balances. Bob, her husband, has pleaded with her to lighten up. The unpaid bills have gotten so out of hand that Helen is being forced to look for a job in order to pay them.

Unable to find suitable employment, Helen had to resort to menial labor, which she absolutely loathes. Now, Helen has neither the time nor the money to keep up her appearance.

Ted normally works out of his home office. However, one weekend he had to fly to his headquarters' office to take care of some business. While staying at a hotel, he found out that outlets for passion are more easily available than he thought. Feeling his wife's absence, he found a "substitute."

Since Ted came back from his weekend trip, he can hardly look his wife in the eyes. In an attempt to numb his conscience, Ted keeps his eyes on the TV and his hands wrapped around a bottle, can, or glass. His

gratification was short-lived, and his future is hazy.

The Big House

Ken and Cathy live in a modest home in an average neighborhood. Although they have a good life and lack very little materially, Cathy is obsessed with getting a big house on the hill. Ken is quite satisfied with things as they are, but Cathy's obsession is getting him down. They both know that they couldn't afford the monthly payments on a new house.

Ken works at a bank and has access to rather large sums of money. Cathy's complaining is driving him to desperation. One day, Ken figured out a foolproof way to embezzle funds from his bank.

After several months of getting away with it, Ken put his earnings as a down payment on a new house. He and Cathy moved in and spent the next several months furnishing and landscaping. At last, Cathy was satisfied that she had outdone her friends and relatives. She could hardly wait to set up some social engagements as an excuse to show off her new house.

Monday morning, while engaged in a flurry of activity, Cathy received a phone call. She was notified that her husband had been arrested. With her husband in prison, Cathy couldn't pay the bills. The big house was sold, and Cathy was forced to move into a small apartment. The apartment was located in another city, for the sake of the children.

Spiritual Plea Bargaining

One minute, the three girls were chatting happily; the next moment, the head-on collision brought their world to a horrendous halt. Anita, Cara, and Heather had been close friends for quite some time; their mothers were also well-aquatinted with one another. The truth of the aftermath was painfully naked—two dead and one almost certain to follow suit.

As the traumatic truth was revealed to the two most unfortunate mothers, hysteria enveloped them. When Anita's mother received word that her daughter's life was hanging by a thread, she decided to make a deal, "If you will let my daughter live, I will quit smoking."

Heather and Cara's mothers wondered why their daughters' lives had not also been spared. One afternoon, over coffee, the two now-childless mothers voiced their thoughts to Anita's mother. The woman proudly explained to the two grief-stricken women about her negotiating powers.

What she did not realize was that God had willed Anita to live before her mother presented her bargain to Him.

Anatomy of Jealousy

Sue, aged sixteen, was a very popular girl. She was involved in many extracurricular activities at school. She dated a number of equally popular boys. All in all, Sue had a pretty nice life.

In Sue's English class, there was a girl named Patti. Patti was on the other end of the social scale. Patti was rather plain looking, quiet, and shy.

Jeff, who sat next to Sue in class, had been asking Sue to go out with him. He got nothing but refusals.

One Friday, Jeff asked Patti for a date and was so pleased by her acceptance that he told some of his friends about it. By lunchtime, the news had reached Sue.

That evening, Sue cancelled her date because of an upset stomach. As Sue sat in front of the television, all the boys on TV began to look like Jeff, and all the girls began to look like Patti. Sue's stomach was doing flip-flops by then. Sue thought, *The nerve of that Patti ... taking my favorite boyfriend away from me! I'll fix her wagon.*

At first recess, on Monday morning, Sue began to circulate a rumor. The rumor was an indirect assassination of Patti's and Jeff's character and morals. By the time the last bell had rung, the lie had been spread all over school. By Tuesday evening, Patti's parents had heard some pretty far-out stories. They told Patti that she would not be allowed to date for a month and that she could never date Jeff again.

When Sue heard the verdict in school next day, she smiled to herself with deep satisfaction. When Jeff got the bad news, he felt terrible.

The following week, Jeff asked Sue for a date. *No* was all she said.

Mind over Matter Does Matter

Many factions are expounding the powers of the mind; some present their case in a very positive manner. While there is nothing wrong with using brainpower, let us bear in mind that our brain was created by someone greater than ourselves.

This precaution will keep us from being too self-reliant, lest we forget to rely on God—"a very present help in time of trouble" (Ps. 46:1).

Check Your Facts

Whenever I need facts, there is a certain well-respected member of our congregation to whom I go. If he does not have an immediate answer for me, he always checks with an accurate source. This character trait has endeared him to me.

The temptation to give a "pat" answer is strong. It is also tempting to give any old answer, just to prove that we are in the know. To overcome these temptations indicates a strong character.

When Jesus needed answers, He went to His Father, the Heavenly Encyclopedia of all knowledge.

Petty Pros

The muscular young man had been the leading hitter on his team for several years. For this reason, among others, he was envied by some of his teammates. Although they were all millionaires, they were not above pettiness.

As the season neared its end, the Christian athlete needed only one more hit to reach his goal. On a controversial play, the official scorer first ruled an error on the fielder. After a brief consultation, however, the ball was ruled a hit.

It is always more expedient to drag another person down rather than lift oneself up. So after the game, several players gathered together to pay a visit to the official scorer. They returned to the dressing room in a state of glee—they had once again gotten the official scorer to reverse his decision.

The next day, the cheated player got a clean base hit to win the game and achieve his personal goal. In the dugout, his "loyal" teammates could only scowl.

Is He Happy Now?

Norman was being lured away from home by all the "swinging singles" propaganda. He had already decided to risk his ten-year marriage and nine-year-old child's future. After a number of blatantly adulterous affairs, his wife threatened to leave him. That is when I met him.

He came into my office, asking my advice—that is, if he should stay with a woman who wasn't filling his needs. I advised him to communicate more with wife and to keep me posted. I could tell by the look on his face that he had not heard what he'd wanted to hear.

During the next couple of years, his lifestyle confirmed my suspicions.

I saw him almost three years later. Upon recognizing him, I asked if he were happier now.

"No," me mumbled. "In fact, I've been thinking about a reconciliation. I'd like to have my wife and child back now."

But the real question is, Will his wife and child want him back?

Provocative Dress

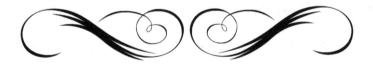

Provocative Dress

A young man sought my counsel recently. Over the telephone, he told me that he had a problem. I invited him to elaborate.

He told me that he had not attended church services for several months and that he would probably never attend them again. I asked him what had prompted his decision. He explained the situation thusly:

"I went to church a few months ago. While I was waiting for the worship service to begin, an attractive female sat directly in front of me. She was dressed provocatively, and no matter how hard I tried, I couldn't concentrate on the service nor could I keep my mind on the Lord. Instead of leaving church in a state of joy, I felt like a worthless sinner."

What advice could I give this perplexed young man? I simply told him to keep on worshipping the Lord and to keep going to church—lest he commit the real sin of giving up his faith.

Reincarnation

Reincarnation

The theory of reincarnation has become increasingly widespread. Even among Christians, it has been the subject of more than a few conversation. The exponents of reincarnation tell us that, after death, we will come back again and again in another body until we have become perfect.

Theories such as this erode the Christian faith. Jesus was the only one who has ever died in a state of perfection. Realizing that He died for our imperfections and relying on His grace to give us eternal life is what Christianity is all about. People who would rather rely on their own thoughts and powers invent theories about reincarnation and other such nonsense.

Revenge

Dying of Thirst

In college, Stan and Eppa were friends. Years later, Stan became one of the top executives for a large chemical company. Eppa was in charge of a government agency. Eppa had given Stan many friendly warning to clean up his act, but Stan was relying on their friendship to avoid prosecution. After the court battle was over, Stan decided to get revenge.

Pretending to still be friends, Stan invited Eppa for a dune buggy ride in the desert. While they were admiring some cactus bloom, Eppa hoisted his canteen. Stan pulled out his gun and put a bullet hole in the metal container of the precious liquid. He quickly jumped in his dune buggy and left Eppa to die of thirst.

Stan drove around the desert for hours, looking for the main road. He could not find it and finally ran himself out of fuel. After walking in circles for three days, Stan decided he was lost. His suspicions were confirmed when he ended up at the site of the shooting.

He crawled over to the damaged container, hoping to find a little of the precious liquid. The last words he uttered were "What have I done?"

Salvation

Unzoned Places

On the edge of New York City

where not too many people go.

I met my Savior

where the four winds blow.

It wasn't in Times Square,

it wasn't under the boardwalk,

or on the Ferris wheel—

I said I met my Savior

where the four winds blow.

To you outsiders, this may sound strange;

but take it from one who knows.

If you wanna find a Savior to call your own,

fly where others haven't flown

And when you reach you destination,

it won't be just a fascination;

it won't be puppy love.

Come and end your destitution

and make a resolution to fly with me—

where the four winds blow,

where the four winds blow,

where the four winds blow.

Advance and Retreat

Let's stop playing advance and retreat;
don't you now the future joy can't be beat?

How many times must we play this game,
remembering when we were to blame?
Don't you know we can all advance?
Come on, people, don't take a chance,
take a chance, take a chance!

This game is strictly a big waste of time;
the winner won't even win a dime.
Eternal stakes can't be any higher
You'd best jump down off your thin wire,
your thin wire, your thin wire!

One of these days, when you are facing defeat,
you'll say, "Why did I play advance and retreat?"
So get on board and grab your shield
and see how good His love can feel, love can feel, love can feel!

No more advance and retreat,

no more advance and retreat,

no more advance and retreat!

"?"

"I hope I get to heaven"—whenever I hear this statement uttered by a Christian, I am amazed.

To be a Christian means to be a follower of Jesus Christ. We would not follow someone in whom we do not believe. If we believe in Him, we must believe everything He has every said.

In John 5:24, Jesus says, "I am telling you the truth; whoever hears my words and believes in Him who sent me has eternal life. He will not be judged, but has already passed from death to life."

While the title of this article is "?," there is no question contained in the words of Jesus—nor should there be any question as to His meaning.

Today Is the Day to be Saved

Many obstacles have been conjured up and placed on the road to heaven. The roadblocks all have one thing in common—they were placed there by people. At various times, we have heard that a certain food or drink would keep us from entering the kingdom of heaven. Whenever we broke these made-up rules, we felt a twinge of guilt.

If there is one thing that would keep us from entering the kingdom, it is guilt. But when we truly realize the full impact of Christ's death on the cross, we then realize our guilt has banished. This realization gives up hope and encouragement at all times.

This truth makes us free . . . free to enter heaven by believing in Jesus Christ, the Son of the One and Only Living God.

So then, obeying made-up rules does not save us. We are saved by believing, with all our heart, in Jesus Christ as God's message of salvation.

(Scriptural reference: 2 Cor. 6:2)

Nice Is Not Enough

Many times, we meet people who are naturally nice and polite. Sometimes, we think to ourselves, *If only I could be so nice. Nice* is defined as being pleasing and agreeable. I wonder how nice Jesus appeared while he was driving out the sellers and money changers from the temple.

If we were to witness such proceedings in the vestibule or courtyard of your church, many of us would be likely to brand such behavior as unbefitting. Jesus was strong enough to withstand all the labels applied to Him by people. He was able to overcome because He knew where He came from and where He was going.

In 2 Peter 1:5–11 we are told,

> Do your best to add goodness to your faith; to your goodness add knowledge; to your knowledge add self-control; to your self-control add endurance; to your endurance add godliness; to your godliness add brotherly affection; and to your brotherly affection add love. These are the qualities you need, and if you have them in abundance, they will make you

active in your knowledge of our Lord Jesus Christ. But whoever does not have them is so shortsighted that he cannot see and has forgotten that he has been purified from his past sins.

So then, my brothers, try even harder to make God's call and his choice of you p permanent experience; if you do so, you will never abandon your faith. In this way you will be given the full right to enter the eternal Kingdom of our Lord and Savior Jesus Christ.

Once Is More than Enough

Several weeks ago, the most beloved member of our church came to the altar for prayer. She had served as a Sunday school teacher for fifty-three consecutive years.

The next day, I called the dear lady to see how she felt. She told me that she had pneumonia and might have to enter the hospital. While in the hospital, she suffered a mild heart attack but was soon released to the care of one of her nieces. While attempting to descend some stairs, she fell and broke some ribs. She was readmitted to the hospital, and two days thereafter, she died.

How could all this happen to such a dedicated servant of the Lord? The answer can be found in the book of Hebrews:

> And just as it is destined that men die only
> once and after that comes judgment, so
> also Christ died only once as an offering
> for the sins of many people; and He will
> come again, but not to deal again with
> our sins.

This time He will come bringing salvation to all those who are eagerly and patiently waiting for Him. (Heb. 9:27–28)

Guaranteed Salvation

About a year and a half ago, I delivered a sermon entitled "And You Shall Know the Truth and the Truth Shall Set You Free."

The sermon had to do with being set free by the truths that are contained in the Bible. For a long time, I've believed that people should follow their own advice. Therefore, during the past year and a half, I have read the entire New Testament, no less than fifteen times. I am *beginning* to understand it.

Due to the insights that are being gained, I can now give you the truth of a guaranteed salvation—what it is and how to get it. I will begin by giving you a list of what will not guarantee your salvation; some of these items may even lead away from it:

1. Obeying man-made rules.

2. Abstaining from alcoholic beverages.

3. Refraining from various forms of amusement and entertainment, including movies and dances.

4. Listening to spiritually oriented music.

5. Attending or participating in church-related social or athletic functions. (I will go even further. You could go to a church every day of your life and still not receive your salvation.)

6. Singing in the choir will not guarantee you a reserved seat in heaven.

7. Ushering others will not guarantee your being ushered into the eternal kingdom.

8. Serving on church boards.

9. Teaching Sunday school.

10. Perfect health will not procure it nor will the lack of perfect health exclude anyone.

11. Giving 10 percent or even giving 100 percent won't buy God's free gift.

12. Not even being on a church staff will assure it.

13. Relying on the Ten Commandments will even prove to be a fatal mistake.

All the aforementioned may make us feel righteous, but the truth is, we are all less than perfect (myself included). How then are we to be saved? Let me share some scripture with you from the book of Luke. To those trusting in their own righteousness and looking down on the rest, He told this parable:

> "Two men went up to the temple to pray, the one a Pharisee and the other a tax collector. The Pharisee stood up and said this prayer to himself: 'God, I thank

Thee that I am not like the rest of men
. . . robbers, cheats, adulterers; or even
like this tax collector. I fast twice a week;
I pay tithes on everything I get.' But the
tax collector, standing at a distance, would
not even raise his eyes toward Heaven,
but struck his chest and said: 'God, be
merciful to me, the sinner.' I tell you, it was
he who went home forgiven, rather than
the other; for whoever exalts himself will
be humbled, but he who humbles himself
will be exalted." (Luke 18:9–14)

So then the first step on the road to salvation is to admit that we cannot save ourselves but must rely on someone else. Who is that someone else? It is none other than Jesus Christ, the Son of God, who came down to this earth in humble circumstances. He was badgered, accused falsely, spit upon, stripped of His clothing, beaten, and killed for our sake. This is the same Jesus who told us that no one can get to the Father but by Him.

If you want to receive the free gift of eternal life, ask Jesus to be your Savior—nothing more, nothing less.

My friends, if you have not received your guarantee of salvation, claim it now. Believe with all your heart, mind, strength, and soul in Jesus Christ, and you will be saved. I guarantee it, and God guarantees it.

Smoking
and
Drug Abuse

A Silent Companion

Joe was what people call a loner; he kept pretty much to himself. For several years, Joe used to travel with a more silent companion than himself. The companion was a cigarette.

Whenever Joe felt alone, he would reach for his companion. His companion shed a little bit of light on dark nights and gave Joe something to hold onto. Nowadays, Joe has a friend. Now that Joe has found his friend, he doesn't need his companion anymore. In case you haven't guessed who his friend is . . . it's Jesus!

But Only with Friends

Al had been upset by the recent turn of events. An Iranian family had moved in across the street about six months ago. They had about six old cars parked all over the place, which presented quite an eyesore. Al had not said anything about it until today. Hassan, his neighbor, had parked one of the jalopies right in front of Al's driveway. Al was blockaded.

Al stormed over to Hassan's and angrily asked him why he was being blocked. He also wondered aloud to Hassan, "Why do you need all these old jalopies for anyway? I thought you people traveled on magic carpets."

Hassan stated in broken English that he was sorry, but he was not yet familiar with all the customs of America.

Al, feeling somewhat sheepish, decided to change the subject, "Do you smoke marijuana, Hassan?"

Hassan quickly answered the challenge. "Sure, sure, I smoke marijuana, but only with friends."

Hassan had made an excellent point. If you're going to smoke marijuana, you had better be among friends. If your enemies spot you, they may decide to turn you in. Of course, sometimes, it's difficult to distinguish our friends from our enemies. Even the best of friends have been known to become enemies.

Betrayed

All three of the applicants were about equal in their qualifications, so they were scheduled for an interview with Mr. Brooks.

During the course of the interview, Karen asked the bank manager for an ashtray. He silently obliged. In the middle of Ann's interview, she also requested an ashtray. Mr. Brooks produced one from the bottom drawer I his desk. Shelley was the third and last applicant for the job opening.

Later, that afternoon, the telephone rang.

"Yes, Mr. Brooks, this Shelly. Yes, I can start work on Monday morning. Thank you for calling."

Rock and Roll Hell

Though the music industry holds much promise for young people, it is not without pitfalls. Through concerts and record sales, young men and women can quickly attain fame and fortune. It should be noted, however, that many of the superstars of ten years ago died before the age of thirty. In almost every case, the cause was attributed to drug abuse. In an effort to reach surrealistic heights, the opposite effect was achieved.

I admire today's young people for their realistic view of our environment. Drugged states are illusionary and temporary; death is final, unless a person knows the truth about Jesus Christ. If the is truth is known, drugs and other pitfalls will be avoided. Success can then be enjoyed longer in this life, while eternal life can then be viewed through the eyes of hope rather than through the glazed eyes of fear.

Cops and Crops

Kona had just devised a new plan for cultivating marijuana. By positioning the illegal plant in the midst of his crops, he could avoid detection.

As the police helicopter patrolled the island, something caught the pilot's eye. In the middle of a small agricultural section, something seemed amiss. The pilot landed the chopper and pushed through the foliage for a closer look. His inspection confirmed his suspicion, and the coast is no longer clear for Kona!

A Broken Promise

Alicia and Judy met during a pivotal point in their lives. Judy was trying to quit smoking, and Alicia was trying to lose some weight. As they worked, each one explained her intentions to the other. It was an ideal situation. In weak moments, one would bolster the other; in lighter moments, the women would joke with each other about their weaknesses.

At the end of two weeks, the women stuck to their promises and became fast friends. Judy was particularly glad to have given up smoking because Alicia was not her best friend. Since Judy would not dream of forcing food on her dieting friend, she certainly would not want to force Alicia to inhale unwanted cigarette smoke.

Over the weekend, however, Judy had a quarrel with her boyfriend; the difference of opinion had left her in a state of depression. She reached for her twenty tobacco-filled pacifiers.

On Monday, Judy approached Alicia with the bad news. As she lit her cigarette, she said, "I hope this cigarette smoke won't bother you too much."

Alicia answered her friend very softly, "Not as much as it's going to bother you."

Coward's Cop-Out

Julio started smoking marijuana in high school just because it was "in." He was already in his twenties when he started experimenting with harder stuff. He saw nothing wrong with his hobby. *It's not hurting anyone, and besides, I can easily afford it,* he thought to himself.

But that was before the "pusher man" upped the price.

Now, in a restaurant, he saw the frail-looking lady heading toward the telephone 'round the corridor. He followed her there.

Before he realized what he was doing, his fist slammed into her head. Surprised that she didn't go down, he punched her again and snatched at her purse. When he encountered resistance, he quickly looked around. Afraid that he might be seen, he did what all cowards do best . . . he ran.

Sleeping Sitter

Natalie had really been enjoying her newfound babysitting job. Sitting for the Taylors was so easy. After putting little Stephanie to bed at eight, she was free to do as she wished. The two dollar per hour seemed easy money.

The Taylors, who left at seven, told Natalie they would return at eleven. By doing some quick arithmetic, the girl's imagination was already spending the eight dollars. She sat down on the Taylors' new sofa and lit up a cigarette to relax. She had sat for the Taylors for the day they purchased the new piece of furniture. She remembered the five-hundred-dollar price tag attached to it.

As she sat there, she became sleepy and dozed off. When she woke up, she could see nothing and smelled the most sickening smoke imaginable.

"The sofa's on fire!" she screamed.

She dropped to the floor and crawled to the telephone and called the fire department. The firefighters arrived within minutes, and only the sofa was lost.

Natalie did some more math and decided she owed the Taylor's a lot of hours' worth of free babysitting.

Child Abuse

Nancy sat horror stricken, as she read the article in the newspaper. It was the story of a woman who had a bizarre way of punishing her child.

Whenever she discovered her son eating or drinking between meals, she would immobilize him with rope. After doing this, the woman would force smoke down his throat. This procedure, she concluded, would teach him a lesson.

Nancy looked across the table at her own son. She thought to herself, *What kind of mother could do such a thing?*

She decided to share the story with her son. Before she could speak, however, she would have to remove the cigarette from her mouth.

Trials

The Heart of the Matter

As John lay writhing in agony, people came to satisfy their curiosity.

"What's your problem?" a passerby asked

"I think it's my heart. Can you do anything for me?"

"Where's your faith? Why don't you trust the Lord for a healing?" the curious man answered before departing.

A moment later, someone else approached. "What's wrong, man?"

"I think I'm having a heart attack. Can you help me?"

"If it's the Lord's will for you to suffer a heart attack, who am I to interfere? Don't you know the scripture 'Do not despise the chastening of the Lord' (Prov. 3:11)?"

After performing his "religious" duty, the "Lord's messenger" went on his way.

Finally, a blue-collar worker rushed to the scene. As the victim lay gasping, the laborer gave the man mouth-to-mouth resuscitation, administered cardiopulmonary resuscitation (CPR), and asked an onlooker to call an ambulance.

Does this story bear any resemblance to the Bible's Good Samaritan? If you check it!

Police Call

It was late at night when the police received the call. It seems there was someone at the corner of Twelfth and Vine causing a disturbance.

Upon arriving on the scene, the police sought to find out the source of commotion. They found a man surrounded by a crowd. People would approach the man with heretofore incurable afflictions. The police watched as this stranger healed the people and sent them on their way.

The police arrested the man on three counts: disturbing the peace, unlawful assembly, and practicing medicine without a license.

The police were surprised to find out that the man had no surname.

Oh! His first name was Jesus.

Dr. Spotless

Jesse had been physically handicapped for quite some time. Because of this, he was able to perform only light duties at work. To insure against malingering, his employer required him to obtain a written explanation regarding his infirmity from his doctor. When even this procedure failed to satisfy his fellow employees, he was sent to a doctor who was approved by the federal government.

Jesse and his personal doctor were both Christians. For this reason, Jesse wondered why their integrity had to be verified by a third party; nevertheless, he complied to his orders.

After a very thorough examination, Dr. Federal told Jesse that he understood the problem.

"It's too bad you can't inherit a million dollars," the doctor kidded him.

"There's no chance of that," Jesse replied. "However, I am hoping to get a book published soon. Perhaps that will be a way out for me."

"Oh, are you writing pornographic books?" the doctor inquired.

"No, I'm on the other side of the fence. I write inspirational literature."

"Isn't pornography inspirational?" the doctor queried.

Jesse decided that any answer would probably be useless.

On the way home, Jesse reflected upon how fortunate he was to have his honesty verified by someone so honorable.

Paper Plague

As the man lifted the heavy load from the conveyor belt, he felt a jolt to the groin area.

Since the injury occurred on the job, a report would have to be filed.

In the office, the supervisor muttered, "This would have to happen when I'm on duty."

Not knowing how to type, he pecked away with two fingers. Shoving the paper across the desk to the injured employee, he told the man to fill in the appropriate blanks.

The combination of pain and unfamiliarity with federal forms proved to be too much for the victim; he inadvertently transposed some of the information.

The supervisor looked at the returned form and mumbled, "It figures, now I have to type it all over again."

Upon returning from the doctor, the injured employee was greeted by his supervisor. "You sure caused me a lot of trouble today, buddy."

Out of respect to his boss's position, the man remained silent. To himself, however, he thought, *It could have been worse—it could have been you.*

Crucifixion of Indifference

No matter how many times I read the New Testament, I am always shocked and amazed at the brutal way that Jesus Christ was treated. People today would probably handle things quite differently.

Not many would openly argue with His teachings; they would simply ignore them.

If He were arrested, His arrest would probably not result in immediate death; the courts could keep the case going for years.

Few would actually drive nails into His hands; however, His hands would be tied by a maze of contradictory laws.

Few would gamble for His robe; most people already have more than enough clothes.

Though nails would not be driven into His feet, He would find His ability to travel somewhat limited.

His crown of thorns would be replaced by headaches unheard of in His time.

Certainly, not many would plunge a spear into his side; the trend is toward keeping one's hands clean.

The final insult would be the same—recognition after death.

True Witness

Too Good to Be True

Bill and Marty rode to work together. Bill's nickname was Smiley.

Smiley had just explained to his carpool partner how he had told his wife that he was going to play pool last night. Instead, he got drunk and spent the night with another woman.

Smiley interpreted Marty's silence as a put-down.

"Listen, Marty, I'm getting sick and tired of looking at your expressionless face. If you were a real Christian, as you claim to be, you would laugh and smile more often . . . like me."

Marty thought quietly before he responded. "I'm sorry, Smiley. I guess I'll just never be like you."

Take My Seat

Bob was eighteen now and was enjoying a vacation in New York. As he and his father were riding the subway, Bob smelled the strong scent of alcohol.

"Hey, pal, how's about letting me have your seat?"

Bob was repulsed by the odor of the drink's words. "You got yourself drunk. Now you can get yourself sober," Bob replied.

Bob's dad heard the entire conversation. "Here, mister, take my seat," Bob's dad offered.

Bob questioned his father, "Why did you give up your seat? It's a long ride, and he's just a common drunk."

"Bob, try to have a little mercy for people," came the gentle reply.

About fifteen minutes later, another intoxicated man approached. "Hey, mister, how's about letting me have your seat?"

Before Bob's dad could respond, his son interrupted, "Here, sir, take my seat."

Bob's dad smiled.

What's Wrong with Pinto?

Pinto lived in a quiet Christian neighborhood. Most of Pinto's friends liked to wear stickers on their tails. You've probably seen some of these stickers: "Honk if you love Jesus"; "I found it"; etc. Pinto's friends would sometimes tease him for not displaying some Christian slogan.

Pinto was rather puzzled because he sometimes saw his friends' bedecked bumpers exceeding the posted speed limit; sometimes, one of them would jump in the front of him without signaling so that he would almost bump his nose.

Pinto decided that the best way to display his Christianity was to keep his bumper clean.

Close Encounters of the First Kind

When a person encounters God, a change of heart is inevitable. This changed heart manifests itself in various ways for various people. I would like to share a few of them with you.

When Moses, who had fled after committing murder, heard God speak at the burning bush, he decided that the time had come to be God's man instead of his own.

While Paul was traveling to Damascus on a mission of persecution, God knocked him off his horse and temporarily blinded him. When Paul's eyes were opened (literally and figuratively), he became one of the most effective proponents of Christianity that this would has ever witnessed.

Because Noah obeyed God's instructions, he and his family were the only people on earth to remain alive after the flood of God's wrath had inundated the earth.

When God chose Zacchaeus's house to spend the night in, its owner volunteered to give half of his possessions to the poor in order to express his appreciation.

Because Abraham was willing to sacrifice his only son, he is known as God's friend. How's that for a title?

When a man possessed by a legion of demons experienced God's mercy, he went through ten towns proclaiming Jesus.

When a man named Matthew heard God speak, he gave up a lucrative and comfortable career as a tax collector in order to follow Him.

When Thomas saw God face to face, all is doubts dissolved into wondrous worship.

Friends

There were about fifty people living at the Alta Loma Manor, a home for the aged. Those who were old enough sat outside and watched the cars whiz by.

Sometimes, Rhonda and Wendy, on their way to school, would bring the elderly people magazines to help them in their long days. Some of the magazines were Christian oriented. Though the people never said much, they seemed to look forward to the girls' brief visits.

On Easter, the girls saved up their money and fixed up miniature baskets of goodies for their senior friends. The girls also gave them handwritten Easter cards with verses of scripture on them. Some of the time-wearied eyes seemed to regain their youthful sparkle.

As they were leaving, one of the older ladies thanked Rhonda and Wendy for all they and done to brighten her day.

The girls asked her if she believed in Jesus.

The lady, in turn, asked them if they believed in Him.

"Yes," they chorused.

"Well," the dear lady responded, "any friend of yours is a friend of mine."

What Makes Jimmy Tick?

Roscoe had done everything he could to make Jimmy mad at him. He called Jimmy names and baited him at school. Roscoe made up untrue stories about Jimmy and spread them around like dust in the wind. Roscoe even stole something from Jimmy's locker.

Although Jimmy suspected him, he would not accuse Roscoe without evidence. In the lunchroom, Roscoe once even tried to doctor Jimmy's beverage. Through it all, Jimmy was quiet but cordial to his antagonist.

One day, in desperation, Roscoe screamed at Jimmy, "Say! What makes you tick anyway?"

"Jesus," Jimmy answered softly.

Actions

I have received information, enjoyment, and inspiration from our pastor's weekly sermons. But nothing he has ever said inspires me as much as the way he and his family live their lives.

The pastor's wife had arthritis in her fingers until plastic joints replaced her natural ones. Nevertheless, she can be found playing the piano or organ (quite well, I might add) every Sunday. There is a look of serenity and contentment on her face, unlike that of anyone else I know.

The pastor's son and daughter-in-law gave up lucrative careers to become missionaries in Africa. They minister to the Maasai tribe, among others. The Maasai are known as some of the most difficult people in the world to work with.

When the missionaries came home during a recent holiday furlough, their son was baptized by his paternal grandfather. Cliché or no cliché—actions still speak louder than words.

Trust

Sly

Active in middle management with a large firm, Terry is jokingly referred to by his associates as Sly. The reason he has earned this nickname is due to the way he narrows his eyes and darts them back and forth whenever he feels that someone is about to hoodwink him. This habit occurs in about every conversation, regardless of the subject or the conversant.

Once, we couldn't help but laugh as we saw him "shoot a Sly" at a suspicious-looking typewriter. Terry looked as though the typewriter keys had surely conspired against him. The man is probably unaware of his habit, but the habit covey a lack of trust.

Sooner or later, we all have to trust someone or something (probably both). We must, of course, be careful whom or what we trust. Thankfully, we can always trust God, without reservation.

CPSIA information can be obtained
at www.ICGtesting.com
Printed in the USA
FSHW02n1319220718
50579FS